GLUTEN FREE
Christmas!

This book is dedicated to all the gluten-free
people out there who had their Christmas
stolen by the gluten-free Grinch.

BECKY EXCELL

GLUTEN FREE

Christmas!

80 Easy Gluten-Free Recipes for a Stress-Free Festive Season

Photography by
Hannah Hughes

Hardie Grant

QUADRILLE

CONTENTS

Introduction

MY FIRST CHRISTMAS ON A GLUTEN-FREE DIET WAS A DISASTER.

I couldn't eat a single thing, I felt like I was an inconvenience to everyone, yet I still somehow ended up getting glutened, meaning that I spent the rest of the day in pain. Not exactly the most wonderful time of the year.

I was 19 at the time and the thought that I could take charge and tell everyone what I needed felt way outside my comfort zone and just a bit 'me, me, me'. Silly, I know. Plus, the fact that I had next to no cooking skills and zero festive gluten-free recipes to turn to for help... it only made things feel even more impossible. So instead I just foolishly told myself, 'I'm sure it'll be fine,' – but you already know how that turned out!

After all, if you make absolutely zero effort to prepare for a gluten-free Christmas, here's a list of the things you very likely won't be able to eat:

* *The turkey (because it's probably filled with gluten-laden stuffing)*
* *Yorkshire puddings*
* *Stuffing*
* *Gravy*
* *Bread sauce*
* *99% of all desserts*
* *Mince pies*
* *Christmas cake*
* *Christmas pudding*
* *Yule log*
* *Gingerbread*
* *Stollen*
* *Panettone*
* *Christmas chocolates*

I could go on, but there's a limit on how many pages there are in this book...

So what does that leave you with when you sit down for Christmas lunch? Basically, a plate of vegetables. And last time I checked, being gluten-free didn't mean simultaneously turning into a herbivore. I didn't say it out loud, but I was most definitely thinking it:

BAH HUMBUG!

Of course, Christmas isn't all about food. For me, it *should* be about spending time together with family who I probably should've seen more throughout the year. But when you're gluten-free, it's very hard to be 'in the moment' while you're spectating others eating copious amounts of gluten while simultaneously asking you why your plate is half empty. Or from an even sadder POV: rummaging through the trash for the packaging of a particular product to find out whether it's safe to eat or not.

Looking back, my experience above is what we call 'learning things the hard way' and you can bet your gluten-free bread savings fund that I never left anything to chance at Christmas ever again.

The happy ending to my nightmare before/ during/after Christmas is that, over the subsequent years, my experience at Christmas has only improved with every year that goes by. Now I've reached the point where not only does my plate of food look normal again, but I also *feel* normal again! Not surprisingly, when you're gluten-free, the best gifts often don't come wrapped and tied with a bow.

Now, I truly feel like I've conquered Christmas and I want to make sure that no gluten-free person ever experiences a Christmas like my first. Nor do I want them to have to go through the years that it took me to reclaim the enjoyment and normality that I once felt before being gluten-free. So that's exactly why this book exists; it is a book which, in hindsight, I desperately wish Santa had brought me ahead of my first gluten-free Christmas.

Throughout these pages, you'll find a sleigh-load of helpful tips on planning and preparing for the festive season, as well as must-have recipes for all the things that would otherwise have to go on 'Santa's naughty list'. Remember the long list of things we wouldn't otherwise be able to eat at Christmas? I now enjoy all of them (and so much more) each year and, with this book, so can you.

You will find recipes for everything from festive bakes to desserts and edible gifts, right up to everything you'll need for the 'main event' with all the trimmings, party food, remixes of festive leftovers, and tons more. And no, you certainly don't need to be an expert in the kitchen, go on a wild goose chase to find the ingredients or have an army of gluten-free elves to pull them off. Just like with my other recipes, you'll find that 99% of the ingredients required are easily available in supermarkets.

My hope is that you can return to this book each Christmas for years to come, especially as this book focuses on traditional classics, essentials and family favourites that even gluten-eaters will love. It'll be the book that never fails to fill the gaps on your plate where all those nostalgia-inducing, gluten-filled festive favourites once sat. It'll bring the sparkle back to Christmas, so you can focus on what Christmas is really all about for you.

HAVE A MERRY (GLUTEN-FREE) CHRISTMAS!

Becky xxx

About

Season's greetings! I'm Becky, I've been gluten-free for well over a decade, I'm a *Sunday Times* best-selling author and there are now over one million gluten-free eaters following me across social media. Welcome to my fifth book, *Gluten Free Christmas*. Though I once played Scrooge in my school's Christmas play, in reality I've always been a big Christmas fanatic. But that all changed when I became gluten-free.

After the disaster that was my first gluten-free Christmas, I stopped looking forward to it altogether. In fact, I was so preoccupied with the nostalgia of past Christmases (where I could eat whatever I wanted without a care in the world) that it felt like I would never come close to getting into the festive spirit ever again. Yes, that's right, I became the gluten-free Grinch.

As I said in the intro, Christmas shouldn't just be all about the food, but for me personally... it really was, if I'm honest! I used to look forward to a full-blown Christmas lunch with all the trimmings (i.e. nothing missing from my plate), Mum's show-stopping desserts, boatloads of Christmas treats and everything else in between. But in the space between one Christmas and the next, that all changed. Any Christmas cheer I had was instantly ousted by the impending fear of being glutened, meaning that not only did I start to dread Christmas, but I was permanently preoccupied with food all day. What did I do to deserve this, Santa?!

However, it wasn't just the mourning of my favourite festive food that felt like a massive lump of coal in my stocking. As many of you might know already from experience, dietary requirements can affect so much more than just what's on your plate. If you're ill-prepared, they can easily make social situations so much more awkward and difficult and/or leave you feeling like the 'problem' or 'the odd one out' – which is exactly how I felt.

So after a few years of festive disasters of varying degrees, I promised myself that I'd take charge and made sure I planned and prepared for the big day as much as I could... even with the basic skills and knowledge I had at the time. Each Christmas, I managed to bring back at least one or two of my festive favourites by recreating gluten-free versions of them, starting with the absolute essentials, then moving onto my (very long) bucket list of Christmas foods I could no longer eat. Little did I know that by doing this over the course of many years, I was basically writing this book.

And though most would imagine that a book like this was born purely from a place of yuletide joy (why else would you write a Christmas recipe book?) it was actually largely fuelled by pure festive frustration! Although this might seem to most like a strange motivation to write an entire book, I know wholeheartedly that every single gluten-free person out there understands exactly where this book came from. Necessity is after all the mother of invention, right?

Fast forward not-far-off fifteen years to today and so much has changed. I've finally reached the point where I can host Christmas at my house, make everything gluten-free in its entirety and none of my gluten-eating guests even notice or care. And guess what? Now you've got this book, you can do the same too, regardless of your cooking or baking ability. It's time to banish all traces of our inner gluten-free Grinch for good!

Don't forget that there are tons more festive recipes on my blog (www.glutenfreecuppatea.co.uk) and also on my social media channels (@beckyexcell). And, of course, you'll find me there all year round too, sharing lots of gluten-free recipes for all occasions.

GLUTEN-FREE CHRISTMAS

Survival Guide

If you weren't already reading this book, my first tip in this guide would have been: make sure you've got great, reliable gluten-free recipes that the entire family will enjoy... but you've already got that part covered! You really are a smart (gluten-free) cookie.

So instead, these tips prioritize bringing back convenience, ease and enjoyment to Christmas. I'm sure we can all agree that a little more of those three things can make a huge difference when you're gluten-free.

So here are 10 of my best tips that I've learned the hard way over many years, that you can use in conjunction with this book.

1. Mix cooking from scratch with festive gluten-free products found in supermarkets.

When I first started a gluten-free diet, there was nothing like the selection of gluten-free products that you'll find in supermarkets today. Nowadays, most supermarkets will stock lots of essential festive gluten-free products like stuffing, gravy, pigs in blankets, party food and even extravagant gluten-free desserts too, so make sure you take full advantage of them.

And though you're more than welcome to, there's certainly no need to cook *everything* from scratch anymore; a mix of cooking from scratch and convenience products can really take the stress out of preparing for Christmas day, allowing you to pick and choose what you do and don't make yourself. These products

make preparing a gluten-free Christmas so much easier and give you more time to focus on the things you actually *are* cooking.

2. Prepare whatever you can ahead of time.

The best gift you can give yourself at Christmas is this: prepare as much as you can ahead of time. That way, you can *actually* get to enjoy yourself on Christmas day... while also being realistic as to what will fit in your oven all at once! That's why I've created a handy gluten-free Christmas checklist over on page 18, which will give you a rough timeline of everything you can feasibly prepare ahead of time, leaving you as little as possible to prepare on the day.

3. If you're attending Christmas celebrations at someone else's house where food will be involved, let them know your needs as soon as possible.

Though this might seem like something that's purely in your best interests, it's also out of courtesy to your host too. A lot of work goes into preparing food for a crowd and nobody likes to be told these things last minute, trust me!

But if your host has little to no understanding of preparing food for a gluten-free person, it can be a little overwhelming for them at first. However, instantly solving this headache boils

down to two simple things: having the right products/ingredients and managing cross-contamination. The first headache can be solved simply by sending your host the links for specific products you'll need. That way, you've already done most of the hard work for them.

And though the second part of the problem (cross-contamination) can seem a little tricky to explain, I've written an easy-to-understand guide to managing it in this book so you don't have to. It's written not just specifically for the Christmas season, but also for those who may be new to preparing gluten-free food entirely. So make sure they've read that section and ideally have a copy to refer to.

4. Take charge and get involved and/or take food with you.

Though this book generally assumes that you're in charge of the Christmas food to some degree (because you must be when you're gluten-free!), if you're attending a Christmas celebration prepared by someone else and haven't given them much warning, it's usually a good idea to take some safe gluten-free food with you. If you weren't able to send your host links for the essential products as mentioned, this is where you can effectively do it for them.

If this is the case, you've then got the option of buying any essential products at supermarkets or using this book to make whatever you'll need yourself, then simply bring x, y or z along with you. Bonus points if you take them over in advance, but if doing so do ensure they're stored safely and sealed, away from gluten-containing products.

Ideally, you'd not only be tasked with getting all the gluten-free bits you need ahead of time, but you'd also be involved in the preparation and cooking of everything from start to finish. That way, you get to inspect it all long before the packaging is permanently discarded, all while keeping a watchful eye on cross-contamination and how it's prepared and served.

5. Don't let cross-contamination crash your party.

Christmas day can be hectic to say the least, so keeping cross-contamination in mind before you even start cooking, right up to serving it, is essential. Preparing Christmas food and serving it up is likely to be quite different to your usual day-to-day routine, meaning you need to be a little more aware of where gluten might sneak in. Fortunately, I've written a festive guide to managing cross-contamination on page 14, so make sure you read that first.

6. Briefly inform your guests (or ensure they're informed) of a little gluten-free etiquette – especially if there's party food involved.

Though you're aware of the risk of cross-contamination, what about everyone else? For most gluten eaters, it's very unlikely they'll have cross-contamination in mind with an entire banquet of food in front of them... unless they've been politely informed beforehand, of course!

Even something as simple as saying, 'the gluten-free food is over here, so make sure no gluten-containing crumbs, food or utensils make their way over here, thank you,' will usually suffice. Having little stickers or signs that clearly label what's gluten-free work well too, as do any other obvious visual indicators.

But of course, you could always make things easy for yourself and...

7. Make your entire Christmas gluten-free.

When one of my followers first told me to do this, I was a little sceptical. Wouldn't everyone be against this? Would my family even allow it?! However, the first time I hosted Christmas at my house, *everything* was gluten-free, yet nobody even thought twice about it.

Best of all, there was no worrying about cross-contamination and I could actually just relax and enjoy myself for the first time in years. It might seem like a drastic change if it's your first gluten-free Christmas, but now you've got this book, it's more than possible. And I promise that none of your gluten-eating guests will turn their noses up at a single thing!

8. Ask your host to keep the packaging from any products used as much as possible.

The answer to the question, 'is this gluten-free?' can always be instantly answered by the packaging. Without it, it becomes a guessing game that you can't win. For example, I've even been told by well-meaning hosts that a plate of way-too-good-to-be-true party food was completely gluten-free. The packaging had already been disposed of but fortunately, having an encyclopaedic knowledge of every gluten-free product at the time, I was pretty sure that no such product existed, so I politely declined. Later, I found the exact product in the supermarket and it was vegan, but not gluten-free...

Also, quick PSA: remember not to just hop on the Internet, search 'is x gluten free?' and then trust the first result you find. The Internet is rife with misinformation, stuff that isn't up to date, or country-specific info which isn't correct for your location. Looking at the physical packaging in front of you is always the way to go.

So whenever dining away from home, ideally (just like you would any other day of the year) you'd always read the packaging before eating and check for yourself first, so if that's at all possible, make sure it happens. But if that's not possible...

9. If you're not sure, don't risk it!

And this is the overall moral of the story, and the answer to any other tricky situations you find yourself in: Christmas should be no different to any other day when it comes to gluten. Coeliac disease and gluten intolerance sadly don't take a vacation for Christmas! If you're not sure if something is gluten-free or can't check the packaging yourself with your own eyes, then don't risk it. No matter what the food in question is, I can assure you that it's most definitely not worth it.

Bringing food with you, as mentioned in tip 4, can help to mitigate some of the risk.

10. Don't forget to enjoy yourself.

For me, the main idea of all of these tips is getting all your ducks in a row so you can relax and have fun knowing it's all taken care of. As I've said before in my books: failing to plan is planning to fail. Yes, being gluten-free might require a little more planning and preparation, but trust me, it'll all be so worth it on the day when you can just enjoy yourself like everyone else.

A CRASH COURSE ON

Preparing Gluten-free

FOOD AT CHRISTMAS

Of course, the same rules apply as they do all year round! But it's important to remember that the festive season can introduce new situations and challenges that may otherwise slip under the radar.

After all, even the tiniest particle of gluten could be enough to make someone with Coeliac disease very ill. Remember: if foods that are gluten-free somehow come into contact with gluten at any point, then the food is no longer gluten-free and is no longer safe to eat. This is referred to as cross-contamination.

So allow me to introduce you to the golden rule:

> **Gluten-free food should not be stored, prepared, cooked or served alongside gluten-containing food, nor should it come into contact with any traces of gluten through contaminated utensils, hands, work surfaces, etc.**

And while the golden rule can sum up this entire guide in one sentence, it's helpful to be specific in practical application. That's why I've broken down the golden rule into five simple actionable steps: source, store,

prepare, cook and serve. Remember, this isn't an exhaustive guide that covers all eventualities, but rather steers you through the most common occurrences of cross-contamination at Christmas.

1. Source

Not surprisingly, gluten-free food starts with gluten-free ingredients! But luckily for us, sourcing gluten-free products and ingredients is easier than it has ever been.

Unlike days gone by, sourcing gluten-free ingredients is as simple as heading to the supermarket. And, of course, the larger the supermarket, the more likely it is that you'll have a wider selection. You shouldn't have too much trouble sourcing all your festive essentials, as most supermarkets will not only still stock their all-year-round gluten-free selection but also have all their seasonal gluten-free Christmas products out too. It's the best selection we get all year by far!

So how do you know what's gluten-free and what isn't? Most supermarkets have gluten-free (or 'free from') ranges which are clearly labelled, and some of the products from their 'normal' ranges will occasionally state 'gluten-free' on the front or the back of the product.

But remember: not all products will clearly have 'gluten-free' emblazoned on the front of the packaging, nor do they actually *need*

to openly state it in order to be considered gluten-free. To tell if a product is gluten-free or not, you first need to check the ingredients list to ensure it doesn't contain any common sources of gluten, such as:

• wheat
• barley
• rye
• oats
• spelt

If the product doesn't contain any of the above ingredients or feature any additional pesky 'may contain' warnings for any of the above ingredients, then the product is considered gluten-free and safe to consume.

Don't forget that, namely here in the UK, products that are clearly labelled as gluten-free can also often make use of ingredients like gluten-free wheat starch, gluten-free oats and even barley malt extract. So long as these products are clearly marked as gluten-free (which means they've been tested to ensure they're below 20 parts per million) they're also considered safe to eat.

2. Store

Now you've got all your gluten-free products, the next step is to store them safely. Why? Because if a gluten-free product or ingredient comes into contact with gluten at any point, it's no longer gluten-free.

Here are three ways to ensure that gluten-free products and ingredients stay gluten-free:

Once gluten-free products are removed from their packaging, **they must immediately be stored separately from gluten-containing products**. This can easily be achieved by using sealed, airtight containers, stored in cupboards or on separate fridge shelves, away from gluten-containing food.

Label any containers or products using stickers that clearly state 'gluten-free' where necessary. It's always wise to label what's gluten-free and what isn't so it's

clear to everyone else in the household. This particularly comes in handy because you should also...

Keep separate condiments and spreads where necessary. If, for example, you butter gluten-containing bread and then put the knife back into the butter, the butter is no longer gluten-free. So it's always a good idea to have separate spreads and condiments (think cranberry sauce) that are clearly labelled as being gluten-free and only used for this purpose.

The ideal scenario here is to have a dedicated gluten-free cupboard, for example, to store all gluten-free ingredients. Or similarly, having a fridge shelf that's purely dedicated to gluten-free products.

3. Prepare

OK, so you're ready to start cooking. If you've ever floured your work surface with wheat flour or cut a loaf of gluten-containing bread, you'll know how flour and crumbs can get absolutely everywhere. That's why any work surfaces used need to be thoroughly cleaned before preparing gluten-free food in order to avoid cross-contamination. It's best to move any small appliances (especially toasters which are literal crumb bombs) and anything where crumbs could potentially hide before cleaning, too.

Of course, when the preparation starts, it's important to use chopping boards and knives that haven't been used to cut gluten-containing ingredients without being thoroughly cleaned first. Ideally, you'd have separate, easily identifiable 'gluten-free-only' chopping boards.

If gluten-containing food and gluten-free food are being prepared in the same kitchen at the same time, the gluten-free food should be prepared as far away from the 'regular' food as possible. Ideally, you'd designate a 'gluten-free zone' in your kitchen that's a safe distance from the regular food, then keep that solely for gluten-free food preparation.

4. Cook

In a nutshell, gluten-free food should always be cooked separately from gluten-containing food. But even with that knowledge, there are still a few crucial dos and don'ts you need to know before getting your apron on:

DO wash your hands before touching gluten-free food.

DO use separate pans and baking trays that have been thoroughly cleaned first (washing-up liquid and dishwashers are fine for this).

DO use separate, clean cooking utensils when cooking gluten-free food.

DO cover gluten-free food tightly in foil and place it on the highest shelf if cooking gluten-containing food and gluten-free food in the same oven (but please see first 'don't' below).

DO use separate small appliances (such as toasters or air fryers) where they may be difficult to clean between use for gluten-free food.

DON'T use a <u>fan</u> oven to cook gluten-containing food and gluten-free food at the same time - it's possible that crumbs etc. could be circulated around along with the air.

DON'T cook gluten-free food in the same oil that gluten-containing food has previously been cooked in.

DON'T put gluten-free food on the same tray or in the same pan as gluten-containing food.

5. Serve

Since you've already worked so hard to do all of the above, it would be a huge shame to ruin it by taking a spoon used to serve gluten-containing food, then forgetting and using the same spoon to serve up the gluten-free food.

So here is some simple serving etiquette that ensures that your gluten-free food stays gluten-free, right up until the finish line:

DO ensure that any utensils used for serving gluten-free food are clean and used only for this purpose. Consider getting colourful utensils that are used for serving gluten-free food only - this will make them easier to identify.

DO use easily identifiable plates to plate up gluten-free food, or clearly label the plates with 'gluten-free' stickers.

DO place gluten-free food as far away from the gluten-containing food as possible when creating buffet self-serving scenarios - ideally on a separate table. This will help prevent rogue crumbs, utensils or food making their way onto the gluten-free plates.

DO have separate, dedicated gluten-free dips, spreads or condiments where necessary, that are clearly labelled. This will prevent guests from dipping gluten-containing food and contaminating the entire dip.

DON'T serve gluten-free food and gluten-containing food on the same plates.

DON'T place plates of gluten-free food right next to gluten-containing food.

DON'T use the same utensils for serving everything.

If you're new to this, then please don't be overwhelmed! But if you're still worried, then guess what? There is an alternate route to all of the above...

If you want to make life easier, you can always follow step 7 of my gluten-free Christmas survival guide (page 13) and make *everything* gluten-free. Throughout this book, you'll find recipes for everything you'll need for a 100% gluten-free festive celebration, and supermarkets will most certainly stock any ready-made gluten-free essentials you may need. That way, there's no need to worry about cross-contamination at all.

Christmas Checklist

As I mentioned in step 2 of my gluten-free Christmas survival guide, ensuring you prepare as much as you can ahead of time is always a good idea. Think of it as a Christmas gift to yourself! So here's a handy gluten-free Christmas checklist packed with ideas of what you can feasibly prepare ahead of time, and when. Of course, the timings on Christmas day can vary depending on the size of your turkey and especially if you're preparing an alternative to turkey entirely; however, it should give you a rough idea at the very least.

October:

☐ Party food can be made and frozen from now onwards.

☐ Yorkshire puddings can be made and frozen from now onwards.

☐ Check supermarkets for new gluten-free Christmas products as they'll start appearing in early October... and sometimes even earlier! These can be bought and frozen now, or just mentally noted for later on.

November:

☐ Stir-up Sunday: The last Sunday before Advent is traditionally when Christmas puddings and cakes (see pages 172 and 56) are made, but don't be afraid to start making them in early November. These improve with regular feeding over weeks and weeks, so it's wise to make them as early as possible.

☐ If ordering your turkey from a local butcher or supermarket, it's a good idea to place your order from now onwards.

☐ Start testing any new bakes as practice ready for Christmas.

☐ Start planning your Christmas Day feast; everything from what you'll have on your plate for Christmas lunch and dessert, to snacks, treats and party food. Have specific products or recipes in mind that you'll use.

☐ Use your plan along with the recipes you'll be making to devise the ultimate Christmas shopping list. You can also add odd bits to it as you remember from now until Christmas.

☐ Prepare meals which can be made now and frozen for next month. When things get hectic in the week leading up to Christmas, you'll appreciate having them! See my fourth book, *Quick and Easy Gluten Free*, for lots of ideas and inspiration.

☐ Stock up on the essentials for cooking, like non-stick baking parchment, extra-large foil, cling film (plastic wrap), kitchen paper, gluten-free stock cubes, gluten-free gravy granules, oil and seasoning.

December:

☐ Book supermarket delivery slots ready for receiving near Christmas Day.

☐ Make a gluten-free gingerbread house (page 40). Though it can last for months, it's best eaten within 2–4 weeks.

☐ If attending a Christmas celebration at someone else's house, early December is a great time to start buying any products you might need to take with you. Some popular gluten-free products can often unexpectedly sell out closer to Christmas, so it's best to act fast. Don't forget that you can freeze any chilled products if they have an expiry date before Christmas, such as party food, pigs in blankets or pork stuffing.

☐ Clear space in the fridge and freezer, which will massively come in handy closer to Christmas.

- [ ] Around 7 days before Christmas, start making any edible gifts (page 72) and decorate your Christmas cake (page 56).

- [ ] Defrost the turkey in the fridge 4 days before Christmas, if frozen.

- [ ] Around 2–3 days before Christmas, start baking anything you'll need on Christmas Day, such as mince pies, yule log or festive biscuits.

- [ ] Around 2–3 days before Christmas, it's a great time to drop off any products you might need if attending celebrations at someone else's house. Do ensure they're kept sealed and stored correctly (away from gluten-containing products).

Christmas Eve:

- [ ] Squeeze in any last-minute supermarket food shopping (or not if you are super-organized!).

- [ ] Defrost any aspect of Christmas lunch that you prepared or bought and froze ahead of time, in the fridge.

- [ ] Prepare dessert.

- [ ] Prepare gluten-free bread sauce (page 118) and store in the fridge once cooled.

- [ ] If the turkey has been stored in the fridge, take the turkey out of the fridge on Christmas Eve to ensure it's at room temperature when cooked the following day.

Prepare the veg:

- [ ] Prepare the red cabbage (page 139) – this could also be done earlier, frozen and defrosted for Christmas Day.

- [ ] Chop and parboil your potatoes, drain, shake (with the lid on!) and, once cooled, cover and store in the fridge ready for roasting (full recipe on page 135).

- [ ] Chop any veg that is to be boiled, and store in pans of cold water.

- [ ] If making the gingerbread stuffing log (page 124) or using it to stuff the turkey/ make stuffing balls, prepare it up to the point that it's wrapped in cling film (plastic wrap) and chilled. Keep it in the fridge ready for tomorrow.

Christmas Day:

- [ ] **7:15-7:30am** - remove the gingerbread or sausage meat stuffing from the fridge and allow it to come up to room temperature.

- [ ] **7:45am** - preheat the oven to 200°C fan / 220°C / 425°F fan and start preparing the turkey (page 114).

- [ ] **8:00am** - begin cooking the turkey and follow the timings and temperature adjustments on page 115. This will ensure the turkey is ready at around 2:00pm.

- [ ] **11:30am** - begin preparing any roasted vegetables such as bacon Brussels sprouts (page 136), sticky maple parsnips and carrots (page 133), roast potatoes (page 135) and the Yorkshire pudding batter (page 143).

- [ ] **12:30pm** - the turkey should be done and allowed to rest covered in foil. Begin roasting any vegetables you've prepared, as well as cooking your Yorkshire puddings or gingerbread stuffing log (page 124).

- [ ] **1:45pm** - begin reheating any elements you prepared yesterday such as vegetables or bread sauce. Start preparing the gravy (page 116) and recruit someone to start carving the turkey.

- [ ] After Christmas lunch has been served, make any last minute finishing touches to any no-bake desserts or begin reheating desserts, if necessary.

GLUTEN-FREE
Guide to Alcohol ✦ ✷ ✦
AT CHRISTMAS

Though I've wanted to include this important info in some of my previous books, I felt it couldn't be more relevant in this one, as Christmas is a time where you might fancy the odd drink or two... or three. Fortunately, in supermarkets the selection of gluten-free alcohol (beer especially) is better than ever. As always, please remember to drink responsibly!

So here's everything you need to know about alcohol on a gluten-free diet:

Which alcoholic drinks are gluten-free?

Spirits, liqueurs, wine and cider, as well as sherry and port, are all gluten-free. Of course, the only exception here would be in rare scenarios where a gluten-containing element has been added to them, though the ingredients label should indicate this.

Where's the ingredients list?

Unlike food products, alcoholic drinks don't necessarily always need to list every single ingredient in them by law (this may vary depending on where you live in the world). While this might sound scary to those of us who have become religious label readers, if any of those hidden ingredients contain wheat or gluten, they should be declared on the label.

What if I want to drink beer, lager, ale or stout?

All of the above will contain gluten so are unfortunately not suitable for a gluten-free diet. Luckily for us, gluten-free equivalents are now readily available in supermarkets, either down gluten-free and 'free from' aisles or adjacent to the regular beer. Over the last decade since I've been gluten-free (in the early days there used to be only one 'big brand' gluten-free bottled beer in existence), I've seen lots of major brands start to sell their own gluten-free versions. Best of all, these are designed to taste exactly like their gluten-containing equivalents, though there is a distinction in flavour depending on whether the beer is made using *naturally* gluten-free ingredients or has instead had the gluten removed during production.

What's the difference between gluten-free beer and gluten-removed beer?

To cut a long story short, truly gluten-free beer is made without any gluten-containing ingredients at any point – therefore, it's naturally gluten-free. However, as it doesn't use common gluten-containing ingredients that regularly occur in beer, like barley, this can of course result in a different flavour.

Gluten-removed beer on the other hand, is made using gluten-containing ingredients, but the gluten is removed later on during the production process using specific enzymes.

Of course, as gluten-removed beer is made using the actual ingredients traditionally used to make beer (which often includes barley), this results in a taste that almost identically matches the real deal. The finished product must then be tested to confirm it's below 20ppm (parts per million) of gluten in order to have gluten-free labelling, as is the case here in the UK and Europe. **However,** in the USA and Australia, these beers are not officially considered to be gluten-free and aren't labelled as such.

So should I drink naturally gluten-free beer or gluten-removed beer on a gluten-free diet? How can I tell which is which?

The reason things can get a little confusing here is because the accepted answer changes depending on where you are in the world. For example, in Europe, gluten-removed beer is considered to be gluten-free and is labelled as such. However, in Australia, a product must have absolutely *zero* traces of gluten detected in order to be labelled as gluten-free – so instead, gluten-removed beers are sometimes referred to as low-gluten beer. So while a bottle of beer can be labelled as gluten-free in Europe, when it travels on its merry way over to Australia, that exact same bottle should then be relabelled as low-gluten beer.

This also means that in the USA and Australia there's a clearer distinction between truly gluten-free beer and gluten-removed / low-gluten beer. Here in the UK and the rest of Europe, there's no overt way of telling the difference as both naturally gluten-free beer and gluten-removed beer are all labelled as being gluten-free. However, when looking at the ingredients, a gluten-removed beer is easy to spot as it will likely state that it contains barley, despite being gluten-free (because, as mentioned, the gluten is removed during production and it will be below 20ppm, fitting Europe's definition of the phrase 'gluten-free').

The important reason that you should be able to identify naturally gluten-free beer and gluten-removed beer is simple: so you can make an informed choice. Most Coeliacs and NCGS (non-Coeliac gluten sensitivity) sufferers find that gluten-removed beer is completely fine to consume, but, of course, some may not find this to be the case. So in short, now you have all the information, the choice is in your hands.

What about mixers?

If you didn't know, mixers are non-alcoholic ingredients in drinks such as cocktails. On the whole, most of these are gluten-free; however, please always check ingredients labels. Some supermarket own-brand colas are not gluten-free as they contain barley. Also, it's always worth checking when eating out at restaurants whether the cola is safe if you're not sure.

GLUTEN-FREE
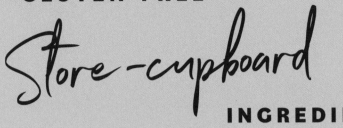
Store-cupboard
INGREDIENTS

All I want for Christmas is all of these ingredients in my cupboards! Why? Well, using them, I can recreate all of my favourite festive dishes, desserts and delights, entirely gluten-free.

Best of all, you'll find that 99% of these products are easily sourced in supermarkets, either in gluten-free or 'free from' sections or among the 'regular' products, but of course you can also find them online too.

This isn't an exhaustive list of every gluten-free store-cupboard ingredient out there, just the ones I use in this book. Happy shopping!

Flour

Gluten-free plain (all-purpose) flour

Unlike wheat flour, gluten-free plain flour is actually a blend of many different naturally gluten-free flours and starches; in *most* cases, it can be used as a substitute for wheat flour. Though not without its limitations, with the right recipes that account for its differences (of which you have loads of in this book!) nobody will be able to tell that the end result is gluten-free.

The gluten-free plain flour I use in this book can easily be found in supermarkets (I used Doves Farm's FREEE flour) which contains a blend of rice, potato, tapioca, maize and buckwheat flour.

But as gluten-free flour is made from a blend of different flours and starches, they vary in their ratios and ingredients depending on where you live. In certain parts of the world,

you might even struggle to find a gluten-free flour blend at all! That's why I've included a gluten-free plain flour blend over on page 205 for anyone struggling to find one.

Gluten-free self-raising (self-rising) flour

This all-in-one flour blend is essentially a plain blend with a little added xanthan gum and raising agents too, though it's not totally uncommon to still add a little extra baking powder for good measure when baking. If you can't find gluten-free self-raising flour where you live, use the simple recipe on page 205 to make your own from a plain (all-purpose) blend.

Cornflour (cornstarch)

This common white starch is priceless when you're gluten-free. For starters, as it's traditionally used to thicken sauces, you'll easily find it in supermarkets – in fact, it's one of the only naturally gluten-free starches that you can find there.

Tapioca starch

Say hello to yet another white starch, but with slightly different properties to cornflour (cornstarch) or potato starch. It's extracted from the roots of the cassava plant and crucially adds a little stretch to your finished baking products. That's why I tend to use it a lot in bread (like in my panettone on page 36) as it's not only incredibly light, but it also adds more of a 'tearable' texture. This is one that you'll likely have to hop online to buy, but trust me – it's worth it! I don't use it a lot in this book, but it's so integral in my panettone that it more than earns its place here as an essential ingredient.

Simple swaps

Ground almonds (almond meal)

The self-explanatory name already tells us why it's gluten-free - it's made by simply blitzing almonds to a coarsely ground powder. Unlike gluten-free flour or even wheat flour, ground almonds have a natural oiliness that ensures your finished bake isn't dry, while also adding a subtle almond flavour. Rather conveniently, it's a staple ingredient in festive baking, so you won't be surprised to find it used in biscuits, frangipane, festive cakes and even macarons within this book. Sometimes considered a gluten-free replacement for wheat flour, when used alone, it has a tendency to make your finished bake very crumbly unless other ingredients are enlisted to counterbalance that effect. That's why you'll often see it used in my recipes in conjunction with gluten-free plain flour, as well as other ingredients that boast binding properties. Do note that ground almonds are different to almond *flour*, which is much finer. You'll need to blitz the ground almonds in my macarons recipe (page 83) before using them.

Gluten-free baking powder

This is a handy ingredient that every baker should have in their gluten-free store cupboards, but I've included it here alongside an important warning: baking powder is one of those tricky ingredients that isn't actually always gluten-free. Some brands of baking powder often add wheat flour to their baking powder to help bulk it out or absorb water. So make sure you double-check the ingredients label of yours first or ensure it clearly states that it's gluten-free.

Gluten-free breadcrumbs

Here's another little time saver that's fortunately available in gluten-free and 'free from' sections of supermarkets. Given that supermarkets are crammed with tons of breadcrumbed products that we can't eat, a small bag of gluten-free breadcrumbs can often equal endless possibilities when it comes to recreating all the foods you truly miss. Of course, you can always make your own by blitzing stale gluten-free bread in a food processor, reducing your food waste in the process too.

Gluten-free stock cubes

Who could say no to a cube of instant flavour? Fortunately for us, there seems to be a wide range of gluten-free stock cubes in supermarkets at the moment. Most of them are clearly labelled as 'gluten-free' but in the UK and Europe don't be alarmed if you see that they contain barley; if labelled gluten-free, they will contain less than 20ppm – the threshold for a product to be considered gluten-free. You can also now find gluten-free and low FODMAP stock cubes online.

Gluten-free puff pastry

This ready-made pastry has been available in most supermarkets for quite a while now, but until recently the true extent of just how versatile it is somehow evaded me. I use JusRol gluten-free puff pastry, which is not only dairy-free, but vegan too – so if using other brands, please make sure you double-check if it's dairy-free or vegan first, if needed. It doesn't puff quite as dramatically as the gluten-containing version, but with the right oven timing, it can emerge quite glorious!

Gluten-free stuffing

Though you're more than welcome to make my extra-special gluten-free gingerbread stuffing log (page 124), buying some classic gluten-free stuffing from the supermarket is an opportunity we never had years ago. You'll want to look for pork sausagemeat stuffing as it's more likely to be gluten-free, but don't forget to head to gluten-free or 'free from' aisles where you might find the 'instant' version too, as well as vegetarian versions.

Gluten-free gravy

Again, you've always got the option of using your leftover turkey drippings to make a quick, homemade gravy (page 116), but sometimes you just can't beat the convenience of a tub of instant gluten-free gravy granules. You'll find these down gluten-free or 'free from' aisles and they're especially good if you're visiting someone else's house for Christmas lunch and need to take it along with you.

There are also a lot more options that pop up during the festive season, such as fresh, ready-made gravy that is commonly gluten-free too.

Gluten-free dried pasta

Gluten-free dried pasta is a like-for-like swap that you otherwise wouldn't need to think twice about. However, the most common variety which is often made from corn, can not only clump together when cooked, but it can be fragile once cooked too, breaking very easily when mixed into a sauce. If you find this too, I'd highly recommend giving gluten-free brown rice pasta a try, which, though a little darker in colour, has no unwanted extra flavour. The main difference is that it doesn't stick together and doesn't break anywhere near as easily.

Alcohol

Not surprisingly, alcohol is important at Christmas... and I'm not just talking about drinking it! So many traditional festive bakes call for spirits, liqueurs and ports, all of which should be gluten-free. Head over to page 20 for more information on safely drinking it.

Binding

Xanthan gum

Acting as a gluten replacer, this ingredient is key to so many of my recipes working as I intended. While it comes in a powder form, once hydrated it has a 'gummy' property that instantly thickens, stabilizes and binds any mixture. Though definitely nowhere near as effective as gluten, it provides all the binding we need 95% of the time.

Despite the unusual name, it's often very easy to source in supermarket free from aisles as it's such a prevalent ingredient in gluten-free baking. A little goes a long way, so we'll generally only need this in small amounts throughout this book.

Psyllium husk

Psyllium husk is to gluten-free bread what gluten is to 'regular' bread. Essential, in other words! Playing a similar role to xanthan gum, this magical powder provides not only a binding effect, but the crucial ability to retain moisture and add a much needed elasticity. Not surprisingly, you'll find this in my panettone recipe (page 36).

Psyllium husk is a form of dietary fibre made from the seeds of a *Plantago* plant. When buying it online, they're either referred to as psyllium husks, whole psyllium husks or psyllium husk powder. All of the above work just fine, just ensure you don't buy them in capsules! Ideally choose one that's labelled 'blonde', otherwise it can have a peculiar habit of turning your finished bake slightly purple! The finer the psyllium husk is ground, the more rise you tend to get on your finished bakes, so ideally go for a psyllium husk powder, if you can. But most importantly of all, please ensure it's clearly labelled as gluten-free, as some can have a 'may contain' warning on them. You can only currently buy this online, but trust me, it's well worth sourcing if you want to make gluten-free bread that tastes like 'real' bread.

Other handy ingredients

Here are all the everyday ingredients that you'll find used throughout this book. While they should all be naturally gluten-free, it doesn't hurt to double-check the ingredients label just in case.

Eggs

Where necessary, I've indicated throughout this book whether you'll need small, medium or large eggs. It can make a big difference, especially in baking! But, did you know that a large egg in the UK is actually bigger than in the USA, Canada and Australia? Because of this, I've included a handy egg 'conversion' guide at the back of this book on page 219.

Butter

One thing I've learned over the years when writing gluten-free recipes is that, once all gluten-containing ingredients have been substituted or removed, the remaining original ingredients become even more integral than before. Case in point: real butter. Not only does it add flavour, but often in baking it adds stability (especially when chilled), structure, moisture and leavening. So if you can use it, please do.

Hard dairy-free margarine or vegan 'butter'

Sometimes called a 'baking block', this is my go-to hard, dairy-free alternative to butter in baking. Unlike margarine that you'd spread on toast, this margarine comes in a hard block, yet despite being a hard block is still softer than butter, so bear that in mind when making pastry or icing. Even if you can't find a hard block of margarine, any hard block of dairy-free or vegan 'butter' should work just fine.

Dairy-free 'buttery' margarine or spread

Thanks to the vegan revolution, the selection of dairy-free spreads and margarine is better than ever, and in most cases you'll find it pretty easy to spot a dairy-free 'buttery' spread. This is the perfect substitution for butter when we're melting it or using it to fry, so I'd always recommend having a tub to hand if you're dairy-free or vegan.

Dairy-free milk

Of course, if you're dairy-free, in my recipes you can always substitute milk with whatever dairy-free milk you'd prefer. Results can vary depending on which type of milk you're using. For example, cow's milk contains lactose, a sugar, which contributes to a golden brown colour once cooked or baked – unsweetened dairy-free milk lacks this property, meaning things may come out looking paler. Be wary of oat milk too that, while dairy-free, won't be gluten-free unless otherwise stated.

Lactose-free milk

My boyfriend Mark is lactose intolerant, so we always have lactose-free milk in the fridge. Lactose-free milk is *real cow's milk*, but with an enzyme called 'lactase' added to help cancel out the lactose. Using real milk or lactose-free milk literally has no impact on a recipe, so feel free to use them interchangeably if you need to.

Greek yoghurt

You might be surprised to find that Greek yoghurt is a staple ingredient when I make any kind of gluten-free flatbread or pizza. It's lovely and thick and full of protein, which binds together wonderfully with a gluten-free flour blend. You can also now commonly find lactose-free Greek yoghurt in supermarkets. Though not used as much in this book as in my previous books, you'll need some for my mini pizzas on page 102.

Garlic-infused oil

This humble bottle of flavoured oil is used in so many recipes across this book, so please head to your supermarket's cooking oil section and pick up a bottle or two! First of all, it adds a wonderful garlic flavour to your dishes without needing to take the time or effort to slice garlic and then fry it. Secondly, if you're also intolerant to garlic like I am, then it's even more valuable. That's because as long as it doesn't have any visible bits of garlic floating in it, garlic-infused oil is low FODMAP and suitable for those who can't tolerate garlic. This really is a wonder ingredient for so many reasons!

Black treacle

Black treacle is basically the British version of molasses. So if you can't find it readily available where you live, feel free to substitute it like-for-like if needed. Mark uses it a lot to create a gluten-free dark soy sauce effect (like in his pigs in blankets chow mein on page 193), but of course it's a staple ingredient in baking anything gingerbread related.

Golden syrup

This is yet another British store-cupboard staple, sometimes known as light or golden treacle. It's essentially a form of inverted sugar syrup with a distinctive 'buttery' taste. You'll always find it with all the other syrups in the supermarket here in the UK. However, it seems to be available all across the world these days, so check the international aisle of your supermarket for it. Trust me, it's worth hunting for!

Flaxseed

Commonly used as a dietary supplement due to its high fibre and omega 3 content, I've included this here for a completely different reason. If you're vegan or egg-free, flaxseed can be used as an amazing egg substitute when baking, especially in cakes, biscuits and even pancakes.

Simply combine 1 tbsp flaxseed with 3 tbsp of water and allow to rest for 5 minutes to thicken. Use as a like-for-like swap for 1 egg.

Minced ginger paste

Minced ginger is one of those magic ingredients that, again, can save you loads of time. Instead of buying a big hunk of fresh ginger that you never finish and have to grate or chop, a little jar of minced ginger is ready to add to your cooking – no chopping required. You can usually find it with all the other spices in the supermarket. You'll need this for my Not-Prawn Toast (page 98).

Spices and dried herbs

A small collection of dried herbs and spices is vital whether you're gluten-free or not. Not only are they incredibly affordable and last a long time, keeping the costs of your cooking/baking down, but they magically transform basic ingredients into memorable meals and bakes.

Think ground ginger for gingerbread, and what would Christmas be without ground cinnamon, ground nutmeg and cloves? Don't forget all those roasting herbs too, like sage, rosemary and thyme, which can either be used fresh or dried.

Food colouring gel (or paste)

I'm very strict on my recommendation for food colouring *gel* throughout this book, not the food colouring liquid you'll commonly find in supermarkets. That's because food colouring gel is highly concentrated, meaning you only need a small amount to achieve an instant, vibrant colour. Not only does this mean you use less and it lasts longer but, crucially, it means you don't dilute your mixture by adding tons of liquid – never a good idea in baking! Plus, liquid food colouring in supermarkets never provides a vibrant colour in cakes or buttercream, no matter how much you squeeze in.

So yeah, hop online and buy a set of food colouring gels and thank me later. I previously used food colouring pastes which still result in perfect colour, but they tend to be a bit more gloopy and require more mixing in; gels tend to be a little easier and quicker to mix in, ensuring you don't overmix things.

Useful Equipment

These are what I'd class as the essentials for Christmas cooking and baking, assuming you have a decent set of sharp knives, pots, pans and a few baking trays already. While not everything is mandatory for this book, if you have all this, then you can basically make everything!

Fan oven

Of course, any sort of oven will do, but I mention 'fan' here especially, as a fan-assisted oven is what I used when testing recipes for this book. However, throughout all my recipes you'll find oven temperature settings for both fan-assisted and non-fan-assisted ovens, as well as a gas mark conversion tool at the back of this book on page 219.

Baking tins (pans), pie dishes and roasting dishes

12-hole muffin/cupcake tray and 24-hole mini cupcake tray

You'll need one of these for all my festive muffins and cupcakes in this book, as well as for gluten-free Yorkshire puddings too (page 143). A mini cupcake tray with small recesses is also crucial if you fancy making the vol-au-vents on page 109 – you can easily find these online and often in large supermarkets too.

20cm (8in) round baking tins (pans)

Though I commonly use two of these tins to make sponge cakes, you'll only need one in this book to make the base for my Neapolitan Baked Alaska (page 156).

20cm (8in) round loose-bottomed baking tins (pans)

Either loose-bottomed or springform baking tins are perfect for making the cheesecakes in this book. I personally prefer loose-bottomed over springform as I find it much easier to get my cheesecake off of the base after, but both work just as well. Also, unlike regular round baking tins of the same size, these tend to have much higher sides.

23cm (9in) and 20cm (8in) square baking tins (pans)

The number of things you can make in a humble square baking tin never ceases to blow my mind. Think brownies (page 198), rocky road (page 196), gingerbread cake (page 68) and homemade fudge too (page 80). Plus, when you slice your creation up, you'll get perfectly square, equal slices. I use both these sizes in this book.

33 x 23cm (13 x 9in) Swiss roll tin (pan)

Though there isn't a recipe *literally* for a Swiss roll in this book, you will still need a Swiss roll tin to make my chocolate orange yule log (page 54), mini yule logs (page 52) and the berry and prosecco roulade (page 154). There's nothing particularly special about it apart from the size, and if you have a baking tray with 2cm (¾in) high sides with the same dimensions, it should work just fine.

23cm (9in) fluted, loose-bottomed tart tin (pan)

Integral for tarts, whether they be no-bake or for creating the perfect shortcrust pastry tart case, ready for a leftovers quiche (page 187), broccoli and cauliflower tart (page 131) or salted caramel pear frangipane tart (page 159).

900g (2lb) loaf tin (pan)

A loaf tin comes in handy during the festive season when you might not expect it – for example, when making my Brie and cranberry nut roast (page 126). They can vary in shape and size – some are wider, which results in a flatter, wider loaf cake that bakes slightly faster. Some are taller, which sometimes means they need a little longer in the oven, so bear that in mind.

23 x 30cm (9 x 12in) rectangular baking tin (pan)

Commonly used for lots of traybakes in my previous books, this tin is my go-to whenever I make something like my sticky toffee apple pudding on page 164. It's not the end of the world if you have a slightly smaller or larger tin; just bear in mind that anything significantly larger will likely result in the end product baking faster or, if smaller, it might need slightly longer in the oven.

33 x 28cm (13 x 11in) ovenproof casserole dish

I recently added a new, larger casserole dish to my collection which is perfect for serving up food to a crowd during the festive period. I use this for my Panettone bread and butter pudding (page 202), potato gratin dauphinoise (page 140) and cheeseboard mac 'n' cheese (page 190).

40 x 30cm (16 x 12in) turkey roasting pan

This goes without saying if you'll be preparing the 'main event' this Christmas, as it's a far larger size than anything you'd ordinarily use the rest of the year. Ideally, ensure it has handles as turkeys can be pretty heavy and the last thing you need on Christmas day is a raw turkey on the kitchen floor!

Ceramic ramekins

These never seem to be a uniform size, but I find that they're all around 10cm (4in) in diameter and anything more specific than that doesn't affect your finished bake all too much.

Essential equipment

Digital weighing scales

I can't emphasize enough how important it is to weigh out your ingredients with digital cooking scales for gluten-free baking. The difference of 10 grams or millilitres can make a huge difference between a workable dough and a wet sticky dough. Unlike baking with gluten, gluten-free baking has very little margin for error, so investing in a digital cooking scale is always a good idea.

Rolling pin

If you intend to take on anything involving pastry or many of the festive biscuits in this book, then a good, solid rolling pin is essential. Mine comes with a variety of thickness ring guides that assist you in rolling your dough out to a specific thickness – utterly priceless!

Non-stick baking parchment

I've learned the hard way that there are definitely different grades of non-stick baking parchment. The cheapest grade still sticks and the more expensive brands are *actually* non-stick! So this might be an area that's worth investing in, as you'll need it a lot for baking.

Mandoline slicer

A manual yet quick and efficient way to slice veg up to be nice and fine (so it cooks quickly) – no electricity required. Larger veg works best with a mandoline and it's very handy to get ahead on veg prep, like for my Mum's red cabbage (page 139) or my potato gratin dauphinoise (page 140). However, please be careful and use the protective grip that comes with it as that blade is very sharp and you can most definitely cut yourself on it!

Foil

You'll need a hefty amount for cooking the turkey and it always comes in handy for lining roasting tins so they're easier to clean afterwards. I also regularly use foil to stop my store-bought gluten-free puff pastry from getting too brown and overdone too, so make sure you've got a generous amount to hand.

Silicone spatula

This is as essential as it gets when it comes to baking. Nothing can scrape a bowl cleaner than one of these, meaning you waste as little of your mixture as possible. It's also essential when gently folding in mixtures to ensure you don't lose lots of air that you've probably worked hard to whisk in. If you don't have access to electric mixers, you can achieve the same result with one of these and a simple balloon whisk. At the heart of all baking, they're all you need – as long as you're prepared to put in a little more elbow grease!

Digital cooking thermometer

I can't emphasize enough how much easier your cooking life could be if you owned a digital cooking thermometer. It's especially important at Christmas when roasting an entire turkey or large joints of meat. Instead of guessing or trying to work out whether the juices are running clear or not, simply probe the thickest part of the meat and you'll have your answer within seconds. Search for 'internal cooking temperature of *insert meat here*' for all the specific temperatures you need to know. It's also handy for testing the temperature of the sugar syrup in my baked Alaska recipe on page 156.

Baking beans

For both savoury and sweet tarts using my shortcrust pastry, baking beans most definitely come in handy. At a pinch, you can always use rice instead, but it feels like a waste of rice!

Electric mixers and cookers

Slow cooker (mine is 6.5 litres / 14 pints)

The winter months are where my slow cooker gets its best use, but there's certainly no reason it can't help to alleviate the traffic your oven no doubt experiences during the Christmas period. While you certainly won't be able to fit your turkey in it, it's great for slow cooking beef (like my peppercorn beef on page 119) or for easy suppers that you can throw on while you're busy preparing for Christmas. They're also considerably cheaper to run than an oven, so make the most of it!

Air fryer

Though not ordinarily suited to cook for a crowd due to their size, air fryers are great for cooking small batches of food super-fast. Again, this can come in handy when your oven is overloaded. If possible, keep your air fryer a completely 'gluten-free zone', as some models can be hard to clean, and cross contamination can be a tricky issue with small appliances.

Stand mixer

Of course, this isn't mandatory for this recipe book, nor is it mandatory for baking in general. However, it can make the difference between baking feeling like hard work or being an absolute breeze. For starters, when making mixtures that require extended periods of mixing (such as buttercream or meringue), you can be completely hands-off. Plus, you can also add ingredients while the mixer is still in motion, which always makes baking an infinitely quicker and easier process. You don't need to break the bank for one, as the power of your stand mixer only really comes into play when mixing dough, which isn't common in gluten-free baking.

Electric hand whisk

Before I could afford to buy a stand mixer, I used a very basic electric hand whisk for all my baking. It mixes just as well as a stand mixer, but of course you're the one who has to put the effort in! For me, an electric whisk still remains the most affordable option for those who are new to baking or don't bake that often, yet still yields extremely similar results.

Food processor

While a food processor isn't mandatory for this book, I can't emphasize enough how it can turn a 10-minute job into a 10-second job. For example, when making my nut roast or Mum's red cabbage (see pages 126 and 139), if I had to slice everything by hand it'd take more than triple the time to achieve the same results. By using the grater attachment, I can shred all the veg required in a flash or use the blade to blitz even the toughest nuts in seconds. It's also very handy for blitzing up biscuits for a biscuit base.

Key

Just as a handy reminder for those still in disbelief: yes, everything in this entire book is gluten-free!

But it's also incredibly important to me that as many people can enjoy my recipes as possible. That's why I've labelled all of my recipes to clearly indicate whether they're dairy-free, lactose-free, low lactose, vegetarian, vegan or low FODMAP.

But even if a recipe isn't naturally suitable for all dietary requirements, watch out for the helpful notes by the key. These will indicate any simple swaps you can do in order to adapt that recipe to your dietary requirements, if possible. If a recipe doesn't state exactly how to adapt it to suit your dietary requirements, that doesn't mean it's impossible! Feel free to use your own knowledge or ask in my Facebook group for advice.

Here's a breakdown of what labels I'll be using so you know what they look like and exactly what I mean when I use them.

Dairy-free

This indicates that a recipe contains zero dairy products. Ensure that no ingredients used have a 'may contain' warning for traces of dairy and double-check that everything used is 100% dairy-free. Of course, if a recipe calls for any convenience products such as gluten-free puff pastry, ensure they're dairy-free. The same applies if a recipe asks for a quantity of pastry from the essentials section – ensure you make that dairy-free too.

Lactose-free

Lactose-free? Isn't that the same as dairy-free? No, it definitely isn't! For example, lactose-free milk is *real* cow's milk with the lactase enzyme added, so while it's definitely not dairy-free, it is suitable for those with a lactose intolerance. The 'lactose-free' label indicates that a recipe is naturally lactose-free or uses lactose-free products. If a recipe calls for any specific store-bought products, ensure they're lactose-free. The same applies if a recipe asks for a quantity of pastry from the essentials section – ensure you make that lactose-free or low lactose too.

Low lactose

I've chosen to distinguish between lactose-free and low-lactose recipes in this book for clarity. In reality, all recipes labelled lactose-free and low lactose (including the swaps needed to adapt recipes if they aren't already) are designed for those with a lactose intolerance.

Low lactose recipes make use of ingredients that are naturally very low in lactose and tolerated well by lactose-intolerants. For example, the production process of both butter and hard cheeses naturally removes lactose from milk, meaning that the end product contains less than 0.1g of lactose. Even mozzarella can contain just 0.2g of lactose. In reality, this means there's often no need to buy a special 'lactose-free version' of these products.

Of course, the use of these ingredients means I don't feel comfortable calling them 'lactose-free' as trace amounts do remain. So instead, I've chosen to call them 'low lactose'. If a recipe calls for any specific store-bought products, ensure they're lactose-free or low lactose. The same applies if a recipe asks for a quantity of pastry from the essentials section – ensure you make that lactose-free or low lactose too.

Vegetarian

This indicates that a recipe is both meat-free and fish-free. Where possible, I've provided simple veggie swaps. Please make sure any products and ingredients used are vegetarian-friendly.

Vegan

This indicates that a recipe contains no ingredients that are derived from animals. Even if a recipe isn't vegan to start with, look out for those little helpful notes for simple swaps at the top of each recipe. While gluten-free *and* vegan baking is a different kettle of fish, if it is easy to make the recipe using vegan alternatives, I'll tell you how in that section. Make sure all products and ingredients used are vegan-friendly.

Low FODMAP

This indicates that one serving of the finished recipe is low FODMAP. The low FODMAP diet was specifically created by Monash University in order to help relieve the symptoms of IBS in sufferers. Brief disclaimer: you should always start the low FODMAP diet in consultation with your dietician. Please ensure that any convenience products you use are low FODMAP.

A few quick side notes: whenever I mention spring onions (scallions) or leeks in this book, I mean the green parts only for FODMAP reasons. Also, garlic-infused oil is low FODMAP too, as long as it's clear and doesn't have bits of garlic visibly floating in it.

Festive
Bakes

Panettone

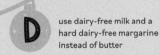 **D** use dairy-free milk and a hard dairy-free margarine instead of butter

 **LL** use lactose-free milk

 V

Serves 8–10

Takes 1½ hours
+ proving time

- 125g (4½oz) sultanas (golden raisins)
- 80g (3oz) candied mixed peel
- 3 tbsp rum or orange juice
- 360g (2¾ cups) gluten-free plain (all-purpose) flour
- 80g (½ cup) tapioca starch
- 85g (7 tbsp) caster (superfine) sugar
- 2 tsp xanthan gum
- 2 tsp gluten-free baking powder
- 15g (½oz) psyllium husk powder (ensure gluten-free)
- 2 large eggs
- 165g (¾ cup) butter, melted
- Grated zest of 2 oranges or lemons
- 50g (⅔ cup) flaked (slivered) almonds
- Oil, for greasing

For the yeast mixture
- 350ml (1½ cups minus 2 tsp) warm milk (around 35°C/95°F)
- 10g (⅓oz) dried active yeast (ensure gluten-free)
- 15g (4 tsp) caster (superfine) sugar

To finish
- 1 egg yolk, beaten
- Icing (confectioners') sugar (optional)

Panettone is something I thought I'd never eat again; if it could be made gluten-free, it would be too complicated. How wrong I was! You'll need an 18cm (7in) panettone paper case, for the full effect, or use a similarly sized springform tin (pan) – just grease it well first.

1 Soak the sultanas and mixed peel in the rum or orange juice. This can be done for a few hours or just the time it takes to do the next steps.

2 In a jug (pitcher), stir together the warm milk, yeast and sugar. Allow to stand for 10 minutes until frothy.

3 Add the flour, tapioca starch, sugar, xanthan gum, baking powder and psyllium husk powder to the bowl of a stand mixer or a large bowl. Mix until well combined, then add the eggs, melted butter, citrus zest, flaked almonds, soaked sultanas and mixed peel (drain off any soaking liquid) and the frothy yeast mixture.

4 Using the beater attachment of the stand mixer, or an electric hand whisk, mix on a high speed for 3–5 minutes until you have a very thick, sticky batter. Allow to rest for about 10 minutes (this gives the mixture time to hydrate).

5 Place the dough in a clean bowl, cover and place in the fridge for 4–6 hours or overnight. In this time it will double in size and reduce in temperature enough to make it easier to handle; around 13–15°C (55–59°F) is ideal.

6 On a lightly oiled surface with lightly oiled hands (you could also do this on a floured surface but I find that can dry it out) shape the dough into a nice rounded ball, then place it in an 18cm (7in) panettone paper case. Cover loosely with cling film (plastic wrap) and allow to prove somewhere warm for about 4 hours or until the dough has reached the top of the case.

7 Preheat the oven to 160°C fan / 180°C / 350°F.

8 Lightly brush the top of the panettone with the beaten egg yolk and slash a small cross into the top, using a sharp knife.

9 Bake in the oven for 1 hour, covering loosely with foil after 20 minutes. Allow to cool completely before optionally dusting with icing sugar. Slice into wedges to serve. After a day or so, the panettone is best served slightly warm – you can refresh each slice by briefly warming it in the microwave.

Freezable: Once cooled, slice and freeze in an airtight container for up to 3 months.

Panettone muffins

 D use a hard dairy-free butter alternative and dairy-free milk

 LL use lactose-free milk

V

 VE follow the dairy-free advice and use a flax egg (see page 27) instead of the egg

Makes 12

Takes 40 minutes

- 180ml (¾ cup) milk
- 1 tbsp lemon juice
- 65ml (¼ cup minus 1 tbsp) melted butter
- 65ml (¼ cup minus 1 tbsp) vegetable oil
- 1 large egg
- Grated zest of 2 lemons
- 200g (1 cup) caster (superfine) sugar
- 1 tsp bicarbonate of soda (baking soda)
- ¼ tsp xanthan gum
- 300g (2¼ cups) gluten-free self-raising (self-rising) flour, plus 1 tsp for the sultanas
- 175g (6oz) sultanas (golden raisins)
- 30g (1oz) candied mixed peel
- 20g (¾oz) flaked (slivered) almonds, plus a handful to finish

If you crave panettone but need that craving satisfied fast, then that's exactly where my panettone muffins come in, being soft, fluffy muffins with all the festive flavour of a traditional panettone. I contemplated calling them 'panettuffins', but couldn't decide whether it was a great idea or a terrible one. The end result is sensational, whatever you decide to call them!

1 Preheat the oven to 160°C fan / 180°C / 350°F. Line each hole of a 12-hole muffin tray with muffin or tulip cases.

2 In a jug (pitcher), mix the milk with the lemon juice and allow to rest for 10 minutes until it curdles a little.

3 Add the melted butter, oil, egg, lemon zest and milk mixture to a large mixing bowl. Mix until combined and smooth, using a hand whisk.

4 Next, add the sugar, bicarbonate of soda, xanthan gum and flour. Whisk by hand until just combined and then immediately stop mixing. Be gentle and don't over-whisk!

5 Mix the sultanas with the teaspoon of flour (to stop them from sinking in the batter), then carefully fold them into the batter, along with the mixed peel and flaked almonds.

6 Spoon the mixture evenly into the muffin cases. Sprinkle some flaked almonds on top of each and bake in the oven for 22–25 minutes until golden and cooked through – check by sticking a skewer into the centre of a muffin; if it comes out clean, then they're done.

7 Allow to cool a little in the muffin tray, then transfer to a wire rack to cool completely.

Freezable: Once cooled, freeze in an airtight container for up to 3 months.

SHOW-STOPPING
Gingerbread House

D

use a hard dairy-free
butter alternative

LL

V

VE

follow the dairy-free advice and use 175ml
(¾ cup) aquafaba (whisked until frothy)
instead of the eggs for the royal icing

Makes 1

Takes 45 minutes
+ 15 minutes chilling
+ construction time

For the gingerbread

- 250g (1 cup plus 2 tbsp) butter
- 150g (½ cup) golden syrup
- 200g (1 cup) dark brown sugar
- 600g (4½ cups) gluten-free plain (all-purpose) flour, plus extra for dusting
- 1 tsp bicarbonate of soda (baking soda)
- ½ tsp xanthan gum
- 4 heaped tsp ground ginger

For the icing

- 3 medium egg whites
- 675g (4¾ cups) icing (confectioners') sugar

To decorate

- 2 boiled sweets (candies)
- Gluten-free small colourful sweets (candies)
- 2 tbsp icing (confectioners') sugar

Unlike most festive baking where the joy comes with eating it, there's definitely an unparalleled satisfaction in making your own gingerbread house and keeping it on display for all to see, for as long as possible. Note that this recipe is totally different from the gingerbread people recipe in my second book; this gingerbread is super-strong, making it perfect for creating edible structures out of. Make sure you check out the tips at the bottom of the recipe before starting as they can save you a lot of time and stress!

To make the templates

1 Grab two sheets of A4 (letter) paper or card, a 30cm (12in) ruler, a pencil (sharpened!) and a pair of sharp scissors, or ideally a small craft knife (use on a scratch-proof work surface).

2 Measure, mark and cut out one 17 x 21cm (6¾ x 8¼in) rectangle and write 'front/back' on it. Measure, mark and cut out one 18 x 18cm (7 x 7in) square and write 'roof' on it. Using the remaining paper, cut out a 15 x 6cm (6 x 2¼in) rectangle and write 'side' on it.

3 Take the shape marked 'front/back'. With one of the shortest sides closest to you, measure and mark 6cm (2¼in) up from the bottom on both sides. Next, along the very top edge of the shape, measure and mark the very middle (it should be 8.5cm/3¼in). Place your ruler from the left mark to the centre mark and draw a line to connect them, then repeat on the right side. Cut along these lines to create the front and back of the house.

Continued...

To make the gingerbread dough

4 In a large saucepan, gently melt the butter, syrup and sugar over a very low heat, making sure it doesn't bubble at any point, or it can ruin the dough when chilled. Meanwhile, mix together the flour, bicarb, xanthan gum and ginger in a large mixing bowl.

5 Add the melted mixture to the dry ingredients and stir together until combined into a dough. Using your hands, bring the dough together into a ball.

6 If the dough is still warm, allow to cool before wrapping it in cling film (plastic wrap) and placing it in the fridge to chill for no more than 15-30 minutes.

7 Remove the dough from the fridge and allow it to warm up a little at room temperature before handling it.

To cut out the shapes and bake

8 Preheat the oven to 180°C fan / 200°C / 400°F and have ready three large baking trays.

9 Place a medium sheet of lightly floured non-stick baking parchment on a work surface and place about a fifth of the dough on top. Roll it out using a lightly floured rolling pin to a 3mm (⅛in) thickness.

10 Use the 'side' template to cut out two shapes, then use the parchment to lift them onto one of the baking trays.

11 Place half the remaining dough on a large sheet of lightly floured non-stick baking parchment and roll out using a lightly floured rolling pin to a 3mm (⅛in) thickness. Use the 'roof' template to cut out two shapes, then use the parchment to lift them onto another of the baking trays.

12 Place the remaining dough on a large sheet of lightly floured non-stick baking parchment and roll out using a lightly floured rolling pin to a 3mm (⅛in) thickness. Use the 'front/back' template to cut out two shapes. Before transferring to the baking tray, cut out a shape for the door (remove, keep and transfer to the first tray) and use a 3cm (1¼in) round biscuit (cookie) cutter to cut out a window hole above the door – only do this on <u>one</u> of the shapes. Use the parchment to lift the shapes onto the remaining baking tray, ensuring all the shapes are lying perfectly flat. Trim any excess baking parchment so it doesn't flap around in the oven.

13 Wrap up any leftover dough in cling film and return to the fridge.

14 Crush the boiled sweets in a small bowl using the end of a rolling pin and scatter the shards into the circular hole on the front of the house.

15 Bake everything in the oven for 12-14 minutes, but remove the tray with the sides of the house after about 10–12 minutes. The smaller door piece should be baked after 6 minutes, so remove it individually to prevent it from becoming dark and overdone. Once baked, allow to cool on the tray for 5-10 minutes, then carefully transfer to wire racks to cool completely. See the tip overleaf for advice on tidying up any edges that have spread too much after baking.

To make the icing

16 I use a stand mixer whenever I make icing, but an electric hand whisk will do the job just fine too. If making by hand, ensure you mix for longer, until everything is well-combined and consistent. Add the egg whites and icing sugar to the bowl of a stand mixer. Starting on a low speed, mix for 5 minutes until you have a thick, smooth paste with a toothpaste-like consistency. Keep covered in the fridge if you don't intend to use it immediately.

17 Transfer half of the icing to a piping (pastry) bag fitted with a small round nozzle (around 5mm/¼in). This amount of icing is enough to glue the house together and pipe intricate detailing on the house, if you intend to; refill the bag as necessary.

To construct and decorate

18 Once cooled, take this opportunity (while the shapes are flat!) to pipe on any detail you fancy. Here are a few suggestions:

• Pipe a fish scale pattern onto both roof pieces.
• Take the front of the house and pipe two squares on either side of the door, then pipe a '+' in the middle of them, to resemble windows.
• Pipe wavy lines along the bottom of the pieces and fill in with icing to create the effect of settled snow.
• For an easy decoration option, pipe small blobs of the royal icing and stick colourful sweets (candies) wherever you like.

19 Allow any icing decoration to fully dry before moving onto construction.

20 To construct the gingerbread house, enlist the help of full jam jars, spices and glass-jar condiments, as these will help greatly. Firstly, have ready a flat surface, such as a cake board, which the gingerbread house will sit on.

21 Take one of the small side shapes and use the icing to pipe all along the bottom edge and up both sides, then stick it down to the cake board. Use a small spice jar to prop it up until it dries. Take the back of the house and pipe the icing all along the bottom edge, then carefully stick it to the front of the standing side and glue down; use jam jars on either side to hold it in place.

22 Repeat with the remaining side shape and the front of the house, using strategically placed spice/jam jars to keep them standing. At this point, the shapes should form a box that resembles a roofless house. Pipe a line of icing all along the long edge of the door shape you cut out earlier – glue to the house as though the door was left open, and support with a small spice jar. Allow to stand while supported by the jars for 30–60 minutes before removing anything you used to support it.

Continued...

23 Pipe icing all along the top edges of the front/back pieces (anywhere the roof biscuit will make contact), ensuring that if any drips, it drips inside the house, leaving the outside clean. Place the first roof piece on top, ensuring that there's a jam jar or similar preventing it from sliding off. Repeat with the other roof piece. Allow to dry with support for another 30–60 minutes.

24 Use the remaining icing to pipe icicles from the edges of the roof or small blobs where more sweets would work. Sift the icing sugar over the house delicately and allow it to settle for a snowy finish.

25 For the ultimate finishing touch, place a battery-powered tea light inside the house. From here on, you can continue developing the rest of the cake board into a festive scene to enhance your gingerbread house, using leftover dough to create appropriately sized people and trees.

Tips: It's super important that you don't allow the butter, syrup and sugar mixture to start bubbling at the beginning of the process. If this mixture gets too hot, the chilled dough can become absolutely rock solid, and will therefore be completely unusable. The more the mixture is allowed to bubble, the more brittle your dough can become too, making it hard to work with. If that's the case, try warming up the dough in your hands a little to make it workable.

As the gingerbread house shapes will spread a little once baked, you can always use your templates and a sharp knife to correct any edges that have become wonky or spread too much. Do this once they've been removed from the oven, but before transferring the shapes to wire racks.

FRANGIPANE OR CRUMBLE-TOPPED

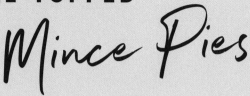
Mince Pies

D use a hard dairy-free margarine instead of butter

LL

V

Makes 12

Takes 45 minutes
+ extra for homemade mincemeat

For a homemade mincemeat filling (or use 1 x 400g / 14oz jar of store-bought mincemeat)

• 200g (7oz) raisins
• 150g (5oz) currants
• 150g (5oz) candied mixed peel
• 150g (5oz) gluten-free vegetable suet
• 200g (1 cup) dark brown sugar
• 2 tsp ground mixed spice
• 1 tsp ground cinnamon
• ½ tsp ground nutmeg
• Grated zest and juice of 1 lemon
• Grated zest and juice of 1 orange
• 1 cooking apple (such as Bramley), cored, peeled and finely chopped
• 50ml (generous 3 tbsp) brandy (optional)

Note: if making homemade mincemeat, the above quantities will make about 900g (2lb). Store any leftovers in an airtight container in a cool dark place for up 1 year. Use in my mince pie mug cake (page 175) or pop tarts (page 70).

In the Christmas chapter of *How to Bake Anything Gluten Free* you'll find my classic mince pies. Here, you'll find two variations I might love even more: frangipane-topped and crumble-topped mince pies. The choice of which you decide to bake is in your hands (as well as if you use homemade or store-bought mincemeat or not) but whichever you go for, you certainly won't be disappointed.

To make your own mincemeat

1 Combine all of the ingredients except the brandy in a large, lidded ovenproof dish. Cover and allow to rest for a minimum of 12 hours. Preheat the oven to 100°C fan / 120°C / 250°F, pop the lid on (or cover with foil) and place into the oven for 2–3 hours, then give it a good stir. Once completely cooled, give it another good stir and then stir in the brandy, if using. Store in a clean jar in the fridge.

To make the pastry cases

2 Preheat the oven to 180°C fan / 200°C / 400°F. Lightly grease a 12-hole muffin/cupcake tin.

3 Remove the pastry from the fridge. If the dough feels really firm, leave it out at room temperature briefly before rolling it. Remember not to handle the dough excessively as you work with it, as this will warm it up and make it more fragile. Lightly flour a rolling pin. On a large sheet of non-stick baking parchment, roll out the dough to a 3mm (⅛in) thickness. Aim to roll out a large rectangle.

4 Use a 9cm (3½in) round biscuit (cookie) cutter to cut out 12 circles for the base of the mince pies. Carefully ease them into the holes of the muffin tin, pressing them in gently. Spoon around 1–2 teaspoons of mincemeat filling into each hole.

Continued...

For the pastry cases

- 1 quantity of ultimate gluten-free shortcrust pastry (page 204)

For a frangipane topping

- 125g (scant ⅔ cup) caster (superfine) sugar
- 125g (generous ½ cup) butter, softened
- 2 eggs, beaten
- 125g (1¼ cups) ground almonds
- 1 tsp almond extract
- 25g (3 tbsp) gluten-free plain (all-purpose) flour
- ½ tsp gluten-free baking powder
- Flaked (slivered) almonds

For a crumble topping

- 110g (scant ½ cup) cold butter, cubed
- 220g (1⅔ cups) gluten-free plain (all-purpose) flour
- 90g (scant ½ cup) light brown sugar
- 1 tbsp ground cinnamon
- 4–5 tbsp icing (confectioners') sugar, plus extra for dusting

For a frangipane topping

5 In a large mixing bowl, cream together the caster sugar and softened butter until light and pale. Add in the beaten egg gradually and mix again until combined. Fold in the ground almonds, almond extract, flour and baking powder.

For a crumble topping

6 With your fingertips, rub the cold butter into the flour in a large mixing bowl until it resembles breadcrumbs. (You can do this in a food processor if you wish.) Next, mix in the brown sugar and cinnamon.

To finish and bake

7 Either spoon frangipane topping and then a few flaked almonds on top of the mincemeat, or sprinkle on the crumble topping. Bake in the oven for 15–20 minutes until golden. Leave to cool before removing from the tin. Dust with a little icing sugar for a snowy finish.

Tip: Mince pie dodgers in the house? Pop some jam in the pastry cases instead of mincemeat beneath the frangipane or use tinned apple pie filling instead of the mincemeat beneath the crumble top.

Freezable: Once cooled, freeze in an airtight container for up to 3 months.

Lebkuchen Hearts

 D use a hard dairy-free butter alternative and dairy-free chocolate

 LL use lactose-free chocolate

 F use lactose-free chocolate and maple syrup instead of honey; one biscuit is a safe low FODMAP serving size

 V

Makes 20–30 hearts (10–20 doubles)

Takes 35 minutes + 90 minutes chilling

- 120g (4oz) honey
- 120g (½ cup plus 1½ tbsp) dark brown sugar
- 65g (¼ cup plus 1 tsp) butter
- 250g (1¾ cups plus 2 tbsp) gluten-free plain (all-purpose) flour, plus extra for dusting
- ¼ tsp xanthan gum
- ½ tsp bicarbonate of soda (baking soda)
- 1½ tsp ground cinnamon
- ½ tsp ground ginger
- ¼ tsp ground cloves
- 110g (1 cup plus 1 tbsp) ground almonds
- 1 tbsp unsweetened cocoa powder
- Grated zest of 1 lemon or orange
- 1 large egg
- Apricot jam (jelly) (optional)

For a chocolate finish (optional)

- 100g (3½oz) dark chocolate
- 1 tbsp melted coconut or vegetable oil

For a sweet glaze (optional)

- 120g (generous ¾ cup) icing (confectioners') sugar
- 2 tbsp boiling water
- 1 tsp lemon juice

I've completely lost count of the times I've seen these cute festive biscuits when out and about during the festive period. However, I'll never lose count of the times I've actually been able to eat them... because that number is zero! Fortunately, this sad fact is made much more bearable with this easy recipe! (Pictured overleaf.)

1 Gently melt together the honey, sugar and butter in a saucepan – but don't allow it to boil! Remove from the heat and mix, then put to one side to cool slightly for 5–10 minutes.

2 Mix the flour, xanthan gum, bicarb, spices, ground almonds, cocoa powder and lemon or orange zest together in a large bowl. Add the melted mixture and mix together until well combined. Add in the egg and mix once more until you have a sticky dough.

3 Place in the fridge for about 90 minutes until a little firmer.

4 Preheat the oven to 160°C fan / 180°C / 350°F. Line a large baking tray with non-stick baking parchment.

5 Roll out the dough to about 5mm (¼in) thick on a lightly floured piece of non-stick baking parchment. Use a heart-shaped cutter (or round, or star, etc.) to cut out shapes.

6 For jam-centred lebkuchen, place ½ teaspoon of apricot jam in the centre of half the cut-out shapes, then brush a little water around the edge of them. Place one of the other shapes on top and gently press the edges to seal.

7 Transfer to the prepared baking tray and bake for about 12 minutes until golden and risen, giving jam-filled ones an extra 2 minutes. Remove and leave to cool slightly before transferring to a wire rack to cool completely.

8 For a chocolate finish, melt together the chocolate and oil (short blasts in the microwave, stirring in between) and then once the lebkuchen are cool, dip them into the chocolate to coat and then allow to fully set.

9 For a glazed finish, mix together the icing sugar, water and lemon juice until smooth and brush onto the lebkuchen. Allow to set.

10 Alternatively, you could also enjoy these without either of the above finishes, as they are delicious just as they are!

Freezable: Once cooled, coated and set, freeze in an airtight container for up to 3 months.

Stollen

 D use a hard dairy-free butter alternative and dairy-free milk

 LL use lactose-free milk

 V

VE see the dairy-free advice and use 1 flax egg (page 27) instead of the egg

Makes 1 large loaf

Takes 20 minutes
+ 40 minutes baking time

- 100g (3½oz) raisins or sultanas (golden raisins), finely chopped
- 30g (1oz) candied mixed peel
- 2 tbsp dark rum (optional)
- 340g (2½ cups) gluten-free self-raising (self-rising) flour, plus extra for dusting
- ¼ tsp xanthan gum
- 1 tsp gluten-free baking powder
- 85g (⅓ cup plus 2 tsp) very cold butter, cubed
- 60g (¼ cup plus 1 tbsp) caster (superfine) sugar
- 1 tsp ground mixed spice
- 50g (½ cup) ground almonds
- 150g (5oz) marzipan, grated
- Grated zest of 1 lemon or orange
- 150ml (⅔ cup) milk
- 2 tsp lemon juice
- 1 large egg
- 2 tsp almond extract
- Icing (confectioners') sugar, to finish

Freezable: Once cooled, slice and freeze in an airtight container for up to 3 months.

Over the years, I've concocted many a gluten-free stollen using wildly varying methods and ingredients, all of which have (thankfully) yielded results just like the real deal. However, what *did* vary was how much time and effort each variation required, with my longest iteration taking 4–5 hours in total. So here's the stollen recipe that I've now decided I will probably use forever; it not only tastes like the real deal, but you can also make it from start to finish in around one hour.

1 Soak the dried fruit and mixed peel in the rum for a few hours or just as long as it takes to prepare the rest of the ingredients. If not using the rum, skip this soaking step.

2 Preheat the oven to 160°C fan / 180°C / 350°F. Line a large baking tray with non-stick baking parchment.

3 Add the flour, xanthan gum and baking powder to a large mixing bowl, then stir to mix. Add the cubed butter and rub it into the flour with your fingertips until it forms a breadcrumb-like consistency.

4 Stir in the sugar, mixed spice, ground almonds, grated marzipan, citrus zest and the dried fruit and mixed peel (drain off any rum, if using to soak).

5 Gently warm the milk in a jug (pitcher), until lukewarm. I do this in the microwave at full power for 35 seconds, ensuring that it doesn't get too hot. Stir the lemon juice into the milk and allow to stand for 1–2 minutes - it should look slightly curdled and lumpy when ready. Next, add the egg and almond extract to the milk mixture and beat together until well combined.

6 Make a well in the middle of the dry mixture. Pour in the wet mixture and work it in using a fork or knife. Keep working it until it forms a slightly sticky dough.

7 Lightly dust a work surface and your hands with a little flour. Place the dough on the surface (it will be sticky, so use more flour if needed) and work the dough with your hands until smoother. Shape into a loaf, about 10cm (4in) wide and place on the prepared baking tray.

8 Bake in the oven for 40–45 minutes until golden, then remove and allow to cool briefly on the sheet before transferring to a wire rack to cool completely. Dust heavily with icing sugar and enjoy cut into slices, cold, or slightly warm if you can't wait.

Mini Yule Logs

 D use a hard dairy-free alternative to butter, dairy-free milk and dairy-free chocolate

 LL use lactose-free milk and lactose-free chocolate

 F use lactose-free milk and lactose-free chocolate

 V

Makes 10

Takes 40 minutes
+ 1 hour cooling

- 2 medium eggs, separated
- 50g (¼ cup) caster (superfine) sugar
- 1 tsp vanilla extract
- 1 tbsp milk
- 1 tbsp vegetable oil, plus extra for greasing
- 20g (1 heaped tbsp) gluten-free plain (all-purpose) flour
- 10g (1 heaped tbsp) unsweetened cocoa powder
- Pinch of xanthan gum
- Gluten-free festive sprinkles, to decorate

For the chocolate icing

- 175g (6oz) butter, softened
- 175g (1⅓ cups) icing (confectioners') sugar, plus extra for dusting
- 175g (6oz) dark chocolate, melted and cooled

Freezable: Once cooled and iced, freeze in an airtight container for up to 3 months.

If you've been missing soft, chocolatey mini rolls, then meet the festive version that you absolutely need to make ASAP. Eagle-eyed readers may notice that the sponge here is totally different to my big yule log on page 54, and for good reason: we need a really thin sponge for the mini version, and this sponge is designed to create exactly that.

1 Preheat the oven to 180°C fan / 200°C / 400°F. Grease a 33 x 23cm (13 x 9in) Swiss roll tin (pan) and line with non-stick baking parchment.

2 In a large mixing bowl, add the egg yolks and half the sugar. Whisk together until combined, then add the vanilla extract, milk and oil and whisk once more. Sift in the flour, cocoa powder and xanthan gum, and mix in until well combined, thick and glossy.

3 In a separate bowl, whisk the egg whites (ideally using an electric hand whisk or stand mixer) until they start to turn frothy. Gradually add the remaining sugar, whisking, until you have medium peaks.

4 In 2-3 stages, use a silicone spatula to carefully fold the egg whites into your egg yolk mixture. Once all the egg white mixture is fully folded in, pour the mixture into the prepared Swiss roll tin. Spread it out gently until nice and even and bake in the oven for 8 minutes until cooked through.

5 Place a large sheet of non-stick baking parchment on a work surface and dust it with icing sugar. While the sponge is still warm, loosen it from the tin and flip it out onto the dusted parchment.

6 Carefully peel off the parchment that was on the bottom in the oven. Don't worry if you lose the outer layer of the cake because it sticks to the parchment as you peel it off, that's totally normal, but do be careful as it's a very thin sponge. Using the dusted parchment, roll the sponge up fairly tightly from a long side, with the parchment inside it as you roll. Leave to cool fully while rolled up. I usually put something heavy against it to ensure it stays fairly tight and doesn't unroll itself.

7 While the sponge is cooling, make the icing. Place the butter in a stand mixer (or in a large mixing bowl if using an electric hand whisk) and mix on a high speed for about 5 minutes, until a much paler yellow. Add the icing sugar gradually (I do this in 2 stages), mixing each addition for 3–5 minutes before adding the next. Now add in the melted, cooled chocolate and mix until fully combined. It should be the right consistency at this point.

8 Carefully unroll the sponge and remove the parchment. I never find the sponge cracks using my recipe, but if it does a little, it doesn't matter – it will all be covered in icing – just be delicate!

9 Spread a very thin layer of icing on the unrolled sponge, leaving a 5mm (¼in) clear border around the edge. Tightly roll the sponge up again (from a long side), but this time stopping halfway. Then, roll the opposite long side to meet the part you just rolled. Next, use a sharp knife to cut right down the middle (in between where the two rolls meet) so you now have two long rolls.

10 Cut each roll evenly into 5 so you have 10 smaller mini rolls – gently squish them to be a bit more round if they have flattened slightly from your cutting. Place them on a board and chill briefly in the fridge (this isn't super-necessary but I think it helps a little).

11 Take each mini roll and spoon a small amount of icing onto each, and spread it so they are all nicely covered. Use a fork or sharp knife to go over each to make a bark-like pattern. Finish with some festive sprinkles and optionally dust with a little more icing sugar.

Chocolate Orange Yule Log

 D use a hard dairy-free alternative to butter and dairy-free chocolate

 LL use lactose-free chocolate

 F use lactose-free chocolate

V

Makes 10 slices

Takes 40 minutes
+ 1 hour cooling

- 100g (½ cup) caster (superfine) sugar
- 4 large eggs
- 2 tsp orange extract
- 65g (½ cup) gluten-free self-raising (self-rising) flour
- ¼ tsp xanthan gum
- 40g (½ cup minus 1 tbsp) unsweetened cocoa powder
- A small handful of chocolate orange treats (ensure gluten-free), to decorate

For the chocolate icing

- 250g (1 cup plus 2 tbsp) butter, softened
- 250g (1¾ cups) icing (confectioners') sugar, plus extra for dusting
- 250g (9oz) dark chocolate, melted and cooled
- 2 tsp orange extract

Freezable: Once cooled and iced, slice and freeze in an airtight container for up to 3 months.

Sadly, a pesky 'may contain' warning stands between me and a lust for a certain well-known chocolate orange treat. Fortunately, this recipe has satiated that craving for many years now and I've never looked back! There are also a few alternative orange-flavoured chocolates available this time of year, which are perfect for adorning your chocolate orange yule log.

1 Preheat the oven to 180°C fan / 200°C / 400°F. Grease a 33 x 23cm (13 x 9in) Swiss roll tin (pan) and line with non-stick baking parchment.

2 In a large mixing bowl, whisk together the sugar, eggs and orange extract until light and a little frothy – I use an electric hand whisk. Sift in the flour, xanthan gum and cocoa powder. Fold into the mixture carefully until fully combined. Gently pour the mixture into the prepared Swiss roll tin, ensuring it spreads right to the edges and is as even as possible.

3 Bake in the oven for about 9 minutes. The sponge should have come away a little bit from the sides of the tin and be slightly risen.

4 Remove from the oven and very carefully invert it onto another piece of baking parchment that's lightly dusted with icing sugar. Carefully peel off the parchment that was on the bottom in the oven. While the sponge is still warm, roll the sponge up from a short side, with the dusted parchment inside it as you roll, into a log shape. Leave to cool completely. I usually put something heavy against it to ensure it stays fairly tight and doesn't unroll itself.

5 While the sponge is cooling, make the icing. Place the butter in a stand mixer (or in a large mixing bowl if using an electric hand whisk) and mix on a high speed for 5 minutes, until a much paler yellow. Add the icing sugar in 2 stages, mixing each addition for 3–5 minutes before adding the next. Now add in the melted, cooled chocolate and mix until fully combined, followed by the orange extract.

6 Carefully unroll the sponge and remove the baking parchment. Spread a layer 1cm (½in) thick of the icing on the unrolled sponge, leaving a 5mm (¼in) clear border around the edge. Carefully roll the sponge back up, as tightly as you can for the best swirl, and transfer to a serving board.

7 Cover the rolled up sponge with the remaining icing and use a fork or sharp knife to make a bark-like pattern. Optionally dust with icing sugar for a snowy finish, and top with some chocolate orange chocolates. Slice to reveal the swirl and serve.

MELTED SNOWMAN
Christmas Cake

 use a hard dairy-free alternative to butter

 LL

V

Makes 20 slices

Takes 5 hours
+ soaking time

For the soaked fruit

The total weight of your dried fruit should be 850g/1lb 14oz. I use the below, but use whatever you have to hand/is available.

- 350g (12oz) currants
- 150g (5oz) sultanas (golden raisins)
- 125g (4½oz) raisins
- 175g (6oz) dates
- 50g (2oz) candied mixed peel
- 120ml (½ cup) rum, plus extra for feeding the cake
- Grated zest of 2 oranges and juice of 1

For the cake

- 225g (1 cup plus 2 tbsp) dark brown sugar
- 225g (1 cup) butter, softened
- 4 large eggs
- 1 tbsp golden syrup
- ½ tsp ground allspice
- 1 tsp ground cinnamon
- 225g (1¾ cups) gluten-free plain (all-purpose) flour
- ½ tsp xanthan gum
- 25g (¼ cup) ground almonds
- 50g (1¾oz) blanched almonds, chopped

For those who are familiar with the Christmas chapter in my second book, the core of this recipe will be pleasantly familiar! I see each Christmas as another opportunity to get creative with flavours and decoration of all our traditional favourites and festive classics, which is exactly what I've done here. With a few alterations here and there, I've perfected a wonderful rum and raisin flavour (which I love in fudge and ice cream) in my traditional Christmas cake recipe and finished it with a very cute melted snowman design on top. He's still smiling despite melting, which I feel has a very deep and meaningful message in it somewhere. Of course, feel free to create your own unique decorations on top too.

1 Place the dried fruit and mixed peel in a large bowl and ensure that any larger chunks are finely chopped (dates especially, if using). Pour over the rum and orange juice, then stir in the orange zest. Cover and leave to soak for a minimum of 12 hours and up to 3 days.

2 Preheat the oven to 120°C fan / 140°C / 285°F.

3 Grease a 20cm (8in) loose-bottomed, deep, round cake tin (pan) and line the base with non-stick baking parchment. Now line the sides too, ensuring the parchment is slightly taller than the tin. Finally, wrap a double layer of baking parchment around the outside of the tin and secure with string, ensuring that the outside parchment is around 5cm (2in) taller than the top of the tin (this prevents the sides of the cake from burning during the long cook time).

4 Add all the cake ingredients to a large mixing bowl. Mix until fully combined, ideally using an electric hand whisk. Gradually stir in all of the soaked, dried fruit thoroughly (including the liquid), using a spatula or wooden spoon. Spoon the cake mixture into the prepared tin, making sure it's all nice and level.

5 Cover the top of the cake with a square of baking parchment with a hole in the middle of it – the hole helps with steam and the covering helps to prevent the cake from burning.

6 Bake in the oven for about 4 hours – it will be a dark golden colour and fairly firm. Remove from the oven and allow the cake to fully cool in the tin.

Continued...

For the royal icing

- 1 medium egg white
- 225g (1 cup plus 2 tbsp) icing (confectioners') sugar, plus extra for dusting

For the decoration

- 5 tbsp apricot jam (jelly), warmed
- 400g (14oz) white marzipan, plus 100g (3½oz) extra for the snowman's head
- 100g (3½oz) black fondant icing
- 25g (1oz) blue fondant icing
- 25g (1oz) green fondant icing
- 450g (1lb) red fondant icing
- 1 edible carrot decoration (ensure gluten-free)

Tip: You can use whisky, brandy or sherry instead of rum if you prefer.

Freezable: Once cooled and iced, slice into individual portions and freeze in an airtight container for up to 1 year.

7 Once cooled, poke all over with a skewer (about halfway down) and spoon over a little extra rum. Remove the cake from the tin and wrap in two layers of baking parchment followed by two layers of kitchen foil. Store in an airtight container for up to 3 months, feeding the cake every few weeks by pouring over 1 tablespoon of rum.

8 Any time from a week to a day before serving, remove the cake from its parchment/foil wrapping and turn upside down onto a serving plate so that the flattest side is facing upwards.

9 For the royal icing, I use a stand mixer, but an electric hand whisk will do the job just fine too. If making by hand, ensure you mix for longer, until everything is well-combined and consistent. Add the egg white and icing sugar to the bowl of a stand mixer. Starting on a low speed, mix for 5 minutes until you have a thick, smooth paste with a toothpaste-like consistency. Cover and set aside.

10 Spread a thin layer of slightly warmed apricot jam all over the cake.

11 Generously dust a work surface with icing sugar and briefly knead the marzipan until softer and more workable. Dust the surface once again and a rolling pin this time too. Roll out the marzipan to a large circle, around 4mm (⅛in) thick, ensuring it's big enough to cover the entire cake and sides.

12 Use the rolling pin to lift up the marzipan and cover the cake with it. Carefully press it onto the top and down the sides so that it's lovely and smooth. Use a sharp knife to trim any excess marzipan left around the base.

13 Roll the extra 100g (3½oz) marzipan into a ball and set aside. Take the black fondant icing and create 3 or 4 balls that you can flatten between your fingers to create large buttons. Create 2 small black balls for the eyes and 6 small balls for the mouth. Use the remaining black icing to create a 4cm (1½in) disc for the base of the hat and the rest for a rounded cylinder with a flat top and base. Set aside.

14 Roll the blue fondant icing into a long sausage shape and flatten to about 1cm (½in) wide. Use a sharp knife to cut multiple, small slits at each end to complete the scarf effect. Roll the green fondant icing into 2 balls. Flatten using your fingers and shape into mittens. Set aside for later.

15 Dust the work surface once more with icing sugar and then roll out the red fondant icing. Roll out to a large circle, around 4mm (⅛in) thick. Brush the marzipan-coated cake with a little water, then use a rolling pin to lift up the red icing and cover the cake with it. Smooth it with your hands, then trim any excess.

16 Place the leftover marzipan ball on top, slightly off-centre. Spoon the royal icing over the snowman's head and into the centre of the cake, then encourage it to drip over the sides in places (like a melting snowman). Allow the icing to set for 10 minutes, then carefully apply the snowman's eyes and mouth to the head, then place the buttons and mittens on top of the cake, leaving ample room for his scarf. Allow to set for 30–60 minutes.

17 Wrap the scarf around the snowman, ensuring it crosses over, and add the carrot nose. Stick a cocktail stick (cut in half with a sharp knife) into the top of the snowman's head and place the base of the snowman's hat on top. Next, place the black cylinder on top to complete the hat.

Dundee-Genoa Cake

 D use a hard dairy-free alternative to butter and dairy-free milk

 LL use lactose-free milk

V

Makes 12–16 slices

Takes 15 minutes + 1 hour 50 minutes baking time

- 180g (¾ cup plus 2 tsp) butter, softened
- 180g (1 cup minus 1½ tbsp) light brown sugar
- Grated zest of 1 orange
- 75g (2½oz) smooth apricot jam (jelly)
- 3 large eggs
- 220g (1⅔ cups) gluten-free plain (all-purpose) flour
- ½ tsp xanthan gum
- 1 tsp gluten-free baking powder
- 100g (1 cup) ground almonds
- 350g (12oz) dried mixed fruit, such as currants, raisins or sultanas (golden raisins)
- 50g (1¾oz) dried apricots, chopped
- 100g (3½oz) glacé cherries, halved
- 30ml (2 tbsp) milk

To finish
- 70g (2½oz) blanched almonds
- 30g (1oz) glacé cherries
- 4 tbsp smooth apricot jam (jelly)

This lighter, booze-free fruit cake is perfect for those who find a proper Christmas cake a little too intense, yet is still overflowing with warming, festive flavours. Being chronically indecisive, I couldn't decide between the classic Scottish Dundee cake or a Genoa cake... especially as they're both very similar at heart. So instead, I made a blend of the two, double-barrelled the name and enjoyed every slice with a cup of tea – another happy ending!

1 Preheat the oven to 160°C fan / 180°C / 350°F. Line a 20cm (8in) deep, round, loose-bottomed cake tin (pan) with non-stick baking parchment.

2 In a large mixing bowl, cream together the butter and sugar until light and fluffy. Mix in the orange zest and apricot jam. Add the eggs, flour, xanthan gum, baking powder and ground almonds and mix to combine. Stir in the dried mixed fruit, apricots, cherries and milk. Ensure it's all fully mixed together and that the fruit is evenly dispersed.

3 Spoon the mixture into the prepared tin, making sure it's level. Arrange the blanched almonds and glacé cherries on top. Bake in the oven for 45 minutes, then reduce the oven temperature to 140°C fan / 160°C / 325°F and bake for a further 65–75 minutes. If at any point the cake looks like it's getting too dark, cover loosely with foil.

4 Remove from the oven and allow to cool in the tin. Once cool, remove from the tin and brush the top with some lightly warmed apricot jam. Once completely cooled, store in an airtight container for 2–3 days before slicing and enjoying.

Freezable: Once cooled and iced, slice and freeze in an airtight container for up to 3 months.

CHOCOLATE ORANGE
Crinkle Cookies

D LF F VE use 2 flax eggs
(see page 27)
instead of the eggs V

Makes 12 cookies

Takes 30 minutes
+ 1 hour chilling

- 60g (⅔ cup) unsweetened cocoa powder
- 60ml (4 tbsp) vegetable oil
- 1 tsp orange extract
- 200g (1 cup) caster (superfine) sugar
- 2 large eggs
- 175g (1⅓ cups) gluten-free plain (all-purpose) flour
- ¼ tsp xanthan gum
- 1 tsp gluten-free baking powder
- 50g (6 tbsp) icing (confectioners') sugar

Freezable: Once cooled, freeze in an airtight container for up to 3 months.

These snowy-tinged chocolate cookies are crisp on the outside yet soft, fudgy and chocolatey in the middle. It's a reader-favourite recipe every festive season that absolutely earned its place here in this book. Don't forget that you could also easily substitute the orange extract for mint extract to make mint chocolate crinkle cookies too.

1 Sift the cocoa into a large mixing bowl, then add the oil, orange extract and sugar, and mix together using a spatula until combined. The mixture should be very thick at this point.

2 Crack in the eggs one at a time and mix between each addition until combined. I do this with my electric hand mixer, but it's more than doable by hand. Add in the flour, xanthan gum and baking powder, then mix until it all comes together to form a soft dough. Wrap the dough in cling film (plastic wrap) and place in the fridge to chill for 1 hour in order to firm up.

3 Preheat the oven to 170°C fan / 190°C / 375°F. Line two large baking trays with non-stick baking parchment.

4 Remove the chilled dough from the fridge and place the icing sugar in a small bowl. Take small amounts of dough (I weigh each portion out individually to 45g/1½oz) and roll each into a ball. Next, roll each ball in the icing sugar and place on the prepared baking trays, leaving room between each ball for them to spread.

5 Bake for 10–12 minutes until they have the lovely cracked effect on top. Remove from the oven and allow to cool on the baking trays for a few minutes, before transferring to a wire rack to cool completely.

ICED CHRISTMAS
Sugar Cookies

D use a hard dairy-free alternative to butter

LL

F

VE see dairy-free advice and use 1 flax egg (page 27) instead of the egg

V

Makes 20

Takes 25 minutes
+ 8 minutes baking time

- 100g (½ cup minus 1 tbsp) butter, softened
- 100g (½ cup) caster (superfine) sugar
- 1 large egg, beaten
- 1½ tsp vanilla extract
- 270g (2 cups) gluten-free plain (all-purpose) flour, plus extra for dusting
- ½ tsp xanthan gum

For the icing

- 3 medium egg whites
- 675g (4¾ cups) icing (confectioners') sugar
- Food colouring gel of your choice

Tip: To make chocolate biscuits, replace 20g (¾oz) of the flour with 20g (¾oz) unsweetened cocoa powder.

Freezable: Once cooled, iced and set, freeze in an airtight container for up to 3 months. Alternatively, freeze the biscuits and icing separately, then defrost and finish.

Sometimes you just need a super-simple yet incredibly more-ish biscuit (cookie) recipe that you can rely on to act as a blank canvas for a spontaneous icing session. And this recipe is exactly that! Unlike a lot of biscuits, there's no need to chill the dough, meaning you can whip up a batch in no time. (Pictured on page 61.)

1 Preheat the oven to 170°C fan / 190°C / 375°F. Line a large baking tray with non-stick baking parchment.

2 In a large mixing bowl, cream together the butter and sugar until light and fluffy – I prefer to use an electric hand whisk or a stand mixer for this. Add in the beaten egg and vanilla extract, and briefly mix. Next, add the flour and xanthan gum and mix until all the flour is combined and it starts to come together as a dough.

3 Lightly flour a large sheet of non-stick baking parchment (and a rolling pin) and roll out the dough to a 6mm (¼in) thickness. Cut out shapes using whatever Christmas cookie cutters you have.

4 Transfer the shapes to your prepared baking tray, ideally using a large palette knife, then bake in the oven for 8–10 minutes until the edges are *very* slightly golden. Bear in mind that larger cookies may need a little longer and smaller ones may need a little less.

5 Allow the cookies to cool briefly on the tray before transferring to a wire rack to cool completely.

6 For the icing, I use a stand mixer, but an electric hand whisk will do the job just fine too. If making by hand, ensure you mix for longer, until everything is well combined and consistent. Add the egg whites and icing sugar to the bowl of a stand mixer. Starting on a low speed, mix for 5 minutes until you have a thick, smooth paste with a toothpaste-like consistency.

7 If you'd like to pipe multiple colours, divide the icing into as many bowls as you have colours. Add a small drop of your desired food colouring gel to each bowl and stir in.

8 Transfer each colour to a separate piping (pastry) bag fitted with a small, round nozzle (around a 2mm/³⁄₁₂in), or simply snip the end of the bag, and pipe away (see the photo on page 61 for inspiration). Allow the line icing to set for 5 minutes.

CHOCOLATE-DIPPED
Shortbread Fingers

D — use a hard dairy-free alternative to butter and dairy-free chocolate

LL — use lactose-free chocolate

F — use lactose-free chocolate

VE — see dairy-free advice

V

Makes 14–16

Takes 20 minutes
+ 20 minutes baking time

- 125g (½ cup plus 1 tbsp) butter, softened
- 65g (¼ cup plus 4 tsp) caster (superfine) sugar, plus extra to sprinkle
- 1 tsp vanilla extract (optional)
- 200g (1½ cups) gluten-free plain (all-purpose) flour
- 50g (1¾oz) cornflour (cornstarch)
- ¼ tsp xanthan gum
- 150g (5oz) milk chocolate
- Gluten-free festive sprinkles (optional)

Tip: Feel free to cut out any shapes from the shortbread dough as you wish, using festive biscuit (cookie) cutters.

Freezable: Once cooled, coated and set, freeze in an airtight container for up to 3 months.

Although I adore this super-buttery shortbread all year round, it's one of those rare bakes that seamlessly carries into the festive period without the need for extensive 'Christmasification'. However, that doesn't stop me from dipping them in chocolate and adorning them with festive sprinkles, something that is factually proven to improve every biscuit or cookie in existence.

1 Preheat the oven to 150°C fan / 170°C / 340°F. Line two baking trays with non-stick baking parchment.

2 In a large mixing bowl, cream together the butter and sugar. Add the vanilla and mix again – I prefer to do this by hand using a silicone spatula.

3 Add the flour, cornflour and xanthan gum and mix once more. Once it's super-crumbly use your hands to start bringing it together to form a ball of dough. It takes time, and you'll think 'it's not coming together, it's too dry' – ignore that thought, just keep going for a few minutes.

4 Once formed into a smooth ball of dough, roll it out between two pieces of non-stick baking parchment to about 8mm–1cm (⅓–½in) thick. Cut out finger shapes, each 7.5 x 2.5cm (3 x 1in) and place on your prepared baking trays. They don't really spread too much so you don't need huge gaps between them.

5 Sprinkle the fingers with caster sugar and use a fork to poke holes down the middle of each. Re-roll the leftover dough and repeat until it's all used up.

6 Bake in the oven for about 20 minutes until lightly golden. Remove from the oven and leave to cool on the trays.

7 For the chocolate coating, melt the chocolate in a small bowl in the microwave, in short bursts, stirring in between. Dip each cooled biscuit into the chocolate to coat one-third, then transfer to a wire rack. Sprinkle with festive sprinkles, if using, and allow to set for 2–3 hours.

RUDOLPH OR CHRISTMAS TREE *Cupcakes*

 D use a hard dairy-free alternative to butter, dairy-free chocolate, and ensure any decorations used are dairy-free

 LL use lactose-free chocolate and ensure any decorations used are lactose-free

 F see lactose-free advice

 V

Makes 12

Takes 50 minutes

For vanilla cupcakes

- 225g (1¾ cups) gluten-free self-raising (self-rising) flour
- 1 tsp gluten-free baking powder
- ¼ tsp xanthan gum
- 225g (1 cup) butter, softened
- 225g (1 cup plus 2 tbsp) caster (superfine) sugar
- 4 large eggs
- 1 tsp vanilla extract

For chocolate cupcakes

- 40g (1½oz) unsweetened cocoa powder (reduce the flour in the base by this amount)

For the Christmas tree decoration

- 200g (¾ cup plus 2 tbsp) butter, softened
- 400g (2 cups) icing (confectioners') sugar, plus extra to finish
- 1–2 tsp vanilla extract
- Green food colouring gel
- Gluten-free Christmas sprinkles
- 12 chocolate stars

For the Rudolph decoration

- 250g (1 cup plus 2 tbsp) butter, softened
- 185g (1¼ cups) icing (confectioners') sugar
- 55g (½ cup) unsweetened cocoa powder
- 110g (3¾oz) dark chocolate, melted
- 24 mini gluten-free pretzels
- 24 edible eyes (ensure gluten-free)
- 12 small round red sweets (candies) or chocolates (ensure gluten-free)

Cupcakes don't get any more festive than this. Start by choosing your cupcake base: vanilla or chocolate. Then choose your icing and decoration: green vanilla icing decorated like a Christmas tree or velvety chocolate icing that bears the likeness of a very familiar red-nose friend.

1 Preheat the oven to 160°C fan / 180°C / 350°F. Line a 12-hole cupcake tray with cupcake cases. (I sprinkle a few grains of uncooked rice beneath each case, as it helps to absorb unwanted moisture.)

2 Place the ingredients for the cupcakes into a large bowl, not forgetting to swap some of the flour for cocoa powder if making chocolate cupcakes. Mix until thoroughly combined (about 1 minute with an electric hand mixer). Divide the mixture evenly between the cupcake cases and bake for 20–25 minutes until cooked through. Check by poking a skewer into the centre of a cupcake – if it comes out clean, then they're done. Remove the cupcakes from the tin and transfer to a wire rack to cool completely.

3 While your cupcakes cool, make the icing.

4 For the Christmas tree decoration, beat the butter until it has turned a lot paler. Add the icing sugar in 2 stages, beating for about 3 minutes between each addition. Once the icing sugar is fully mixed in, add the vanilla extract and a small drop of green food colouring gel, then mix to fully combine.

5 Use a piping (pastry) bag with an open star nozzle to pipe the icing on nice and tall, then decorate with strategically placed festive sprinkles to look like baubles, a dusting of icing sugar to look like snow, and a star to top each.

6 For the Rudolph decoration, beat the butter and icing sugar until the butter has turned a lot paler, then sift in the cocoa powder and mix again until fully combined. Add in the slightly cooled, melted chocolate and mix well until fully incorporated. If the icing seems too thick, just add a teaspoon or so of milk (dairy-free if necessary) to loosen it up.

7 Use a piping bag with an open star nozzle to pipe the icing on nice and tall, then push a couple of pretzels in for the antlers, along with two edible eyes and a red sweet or chocolate for the nose.

Freezable: Once cooled and iced, freeze in an airtight container for up to 3 months. Alternatively, freeze the cupcakes and icing separately, then defrost and finish later.

NO-BAKE
Christmas Wreath

D — use a hard dairy-free alternative to butter, dairy-free chocolate, and ensure any decorations used are dairy-free

LL — use lactose-free chocolate and ensure any decorations used are lactose-free

F — see lactose-free advice

VE — see dairy-free advice and use vegan marshmallows

V — use veggie-friendly marshmallows

Serves 10

Takes 15 minutes
+ 1 hour cooling

- 200g (7oz) marshmallows
- 45g (3 tbsp plus 1 tsp) butter
- Green food colouring gel
- 180g (6½oz) gluten-free rice crispy cereal
- Gluten-free festive sprinkles and sweets (candies), to decorate

Freezable: Once set, slice and freeze in an airtight container for up to 3 months.

Hands up if you agree with me here: the humble rice crispy cake needs to be present at all special occasions, Christmas included. So consider this me sneaking it in, hoping it catches on and I can take the credit for it. Coloured a wonderful shade of festive green, this wreath not only looks the part but is easily sliceable and incredibly more-ish. Just don't hang it on your door or the neighbours might not send you a card this year.

1 Lay a large sheet of non-stick baking parchment on your work surface and draw a circle around a large dinner plate (mine was about 25cm/10in in diameter). Flip the paper so the ink/pencil is on the other side.

2 Place the marshmallows and butter in a large saucepan and allow to melt over a low heat, stirring so it doesn't stick to the bottom of your pan.

3 Once smooth and very sticky, add a few drops of green food colouring and mix it in so it's a vibrant green colour, then remove from the heat, add the rice cereal to the pan and stir until well coated. If the saucepan is too small to cope with this, transfer into a large bowl and mix.

4 Spoon out the mixture into the circle shape you drew onto the baking parchment. It is sticky so just keep your hands slightly wet, which helps you to mould the mixture into shape and push it all together. Once shaped into a compact wreath shape, allow to set for 1 hour before decorating with gluten-free sprinkles and sweets.

5 Transfer to a serving plate, cut into slices and enjoy.

OLD-SCHOOL

Gingerbread Cake

D — use dairy-free margarine instead of butter and dairy-free milk

LL — use lactose-free milk

V

VE — see dairy-free advice and use 1 flax egg (see page 27) instead of the egg

Makes 9 slices

Takes 10 minutes
+ 40 minutes baking time

- 100g (½ cup minus 1 tbsp) butter, softened
- 100g (½ cup) caster (superfine) sugar
- 1 large egg
- 200ml (¾ cup plus 1½ tbsp) black treacle
- 50ml (3½ tbsp) golden syrup
- 275g (2 cups) gluten-free plain (all-purpose) flour
- ½ tsp xanthan gum
- 1 tsp bicarbonate of soda (baking soda)
- 2 tsp ground ginger
- 1 tsp ground cinnamon
- 225ml (1 cup minus 1 tbsp) milk
- 3 tbsp icing (confectioners') sugar, for dusting

Freezable: Once cooled, slice and freeze in an airtight container for up to 3 months.

If you love gingerbread biscuits and/or cake, then this combination of both will be right up your street! It's still every bit as sweet, warming and fiery as you'd expect, but with a super-fluffy, light crumb that's incredibly more-ish – so much so that this humble cake doesn't really even need any decoration or accompaniment.

1 Preheat the oven to 160°C fan / 180°C / 350°F. Grease a 23cm (9in) square baking tin (pan) and line with non-stick baking parchment.

2 In a large mixing bowl, cream together the butter and sugar until light and fluffy – I prefer to use an electric hand whisk or a stand mixer for this. Add the egg, then mix in until combined, followed by the black treacle and golden syrup. Mix until smooth and consistent.

3 In a separate, medium-sized mixing bowl, stir together the flour, xanthan gum, bicarb, ginger and cinnamon. Add half the flour mixture to the large mixing bowl and mix in. Follow this by mixing in half the milk, then repeat with the remaining flour and milk until combined and smooth.

4 Spoon the cake mixture into the prepared tin, ensuring that it's nice and level. Bake in the oven for 40 minutes until cooked through. Check by poking a skewer into the centre – if it comes out clean, then it's done. Allow to cool completely in the tin.

5 Once cool, dust with icing sugar then remove from the tin. Slice and serve with a little gluten-free custard. Alternatively, use the entire cake to make gingerbread stuffing (page 124).

Cinnamon Crescent Biscuits

 use a hard dairy-free alternative to butter

Makes 40-45

Takes 30 minutes
+ 1 hour chilling

- 175g (1⅓ cups) gluten-free plain (all-purpose) flour
- ½ tsp xanthan gum
- 125g (½ cup plus 1 tbsp) cold butter, cubed
- 2 tsp ground cinnamon
- 80g (¾ cup) ground almonds or ground hazelnuts
- 70g (½ cup) icing (confectioners') sugar, plus extra for dusting
- 1 egg yolk
- 1 tsp vanilla extract

Freezable: Once cooled, freeze in an airtight container for up to 3 months.

I absolutely had to recreate these traditional, festive-spiced biscuits I once tried at a German Christmas market many moons ago. Each bite is nutty and warming, with a satisfying snap and a sweet aftertaste of snowy icing sugar. Perfect alongside a warming drink!

1 Place the flour, xanthan gum and butter in a large mixing bowl. Using your fingertips, rub in the butter to form a breadcrumb-like consistency. Stir through the cinnamon and ground nuts, followed by the icing sugar, mixing so that it's well distributed.

2 Mix in the egg yolk and vanilla so that it starts to come together. Finally, get your hands in and bring it together into a dough. Cover and chill in the fridge for 1 hour.

3 Preheat the oven to 160°C fan / 180°C / 350°F. Line a large baking tray with non-stick baking parchment.

4 Use a teaspoon to take portions of the dough, then roll each into a long sausage shape (about 6cm/2¼in long and thicker in the middle, tapering down to pointed ends) then bring each round into a crescent shape, placing them on the prepared baking tray.

5 Bake for 12-14 minutes, then remove from the oven and leave to cool for 5 minutes on the baking tray before transferring to a wire rack. Dust the tops of the cookies with icing sugar and leave to cool completely.

MINCE PIE
Pop Tarts

D   LL   V

Makes 6

Takes 40 minutes

- 1 quantity of ultimate gluten-free shortcrust pastry (page 204)
- 1 egg, beaten
- 6 tbsp mincemeat (see page 46 for homemade)

For the icing

- 200g (scant 1½ cups) icing (confectioners') sugar
- 1 tsp vanilla extract
- 1–2 tbsp water
- Small handful of gluten-free festive sprinkles

Tip: You could also easily make these using a store-bought roll of gluten-free puff pastry. Feel free to swap the mincemeat for tinned apple pie filling too, to cater for any mince pie dodgers.

Freezable: Once cooled, iced and set, freeze in an airtight container for up to 3 months.

What could possibly be better than mince pies in pop tart form? In my opinion, these are not only the most adventurous way to enjoy a mince pie, but also the most underrated. After all, when you've got golden, flaky, buttery pastry, sticky mincemeat and a sweet vanilla icing with crunchy sprinkles, nobody will ever turn them down.

1 If the chilled pastry dough is quite firm, bring it to room temperature and set aside.

2 Preheat the oven to 160°C fan / 180°C / 350°F. Line a large baking tray with non-stick baking parchment.

3 Lightly flour a rolling pin. Roll out the dough to a rectangle, about 2mm (⅛in) thick. Cut out 12 rectangles of pastry, each 10 x 7.5cm (4 x 3in).

4 Brush around the border of half of the rectangles with beaten egg, then add a tablespoon or so of mincemeat. Spread it out, leaving a 1cm (½in) clear border around the edge. Using a fork, prick some holes in the remaining rectangles (to allow steam to escape when baking). Place these rectangles on top of the mincemeat, gently press the edges to seal, then crimp the edges with a fork. Transfer to the prepared baking tray.

5 Brush the top of each with the beaten egg and bake in the oven for 20–25 minutes until golden. Remove from the oven and allow to cool.

6 For the icing, place the icing sugar in a bowl, add the vanilla extract, then spoon in the water a little at a time until you have a very thick icing. You'll probably only need a couple of tablespoons at most. Make sure you mix it thoroughly between each addition so you don't add too much. If it does become too thin, just add more icing sugar.

7 Once cooled, drizzle the icing onto each pop tart. Add a few festive sprinkles and repeat until you've decorated all of your pop tarts. Allow to set and enjoy.

Edible Gifts

Cranberry Pistachio Biscotti

 D use a hard dairy-free alternative to butter

 LL

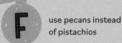 **F** use pecans instead of pistachios

 V

Makes 16–20

Takes 1 hour 20 minutes

- 265g (2 cups) gluten-free plain (all-purpose) flour, plus extra for dusting
- ¼ tsp xanthan gum
- 150g (¾ cup) caster (superfine) sugar
- 25g (¼ cup) ground almonds
- 2 tsp gluten-free baking powder
- Pinch of salt
- 2 large eggs
- 55g (¼ cup minus 1 tsp) butter, melted
- ½ tsp vanilla extract
- 150g (5oz) shelled pistachios
- 50g (1¾oz) dried cranberries

Freezable: Once cooled, freeze in an airtight container for up to 3 months.

I didn't realize the true extent of my love for biscotti until I baked (and subsequently inhaled) this festive version of the classic Italian almond biscuit. Each bite is nutty, sweet, chunky, crunchy and with a welcome hint of almonds and vanilla flowing through it. I'm not sure I even need to say it anymore, but I will anyway: you'd never know in a million years that they're gluten-free!

1 Preheat the oven to 160°C fan / 180°C / 350°F. Line a large baking tray with non-stick parchment.

2 Place the flour, xanthan gum, sugar, ground almonds, baking powder and salt in a large mixing bowl and briefly mix together.

3 Add the eggs, melted butter and vanilla and mix once more – I prefer to use an electric hand whisk or a stand mixer for this. Add the pistachios and dried cranberries and mix until just combined.

4 Turn the dough out onto a lightly floured surface. Briefly knead so the dough comes together and is fairly smooth, then cut into two equal pieces. Shape each half with your hands to form a rectangle about 7 x 13cm (2¾ x 5¼in) and about 3cm (1¼in) thick. Place on your prepared baking tray, leaving a little space between the rectangles, as they will spread a little.

5 Bake in the oven for about 30 minutes, until lightly browned and with a few cracks on the outside. Remove from the oven, leave to cool for a few minutes on the baking tray, then transfer to a wire rack to cool completely. Reduce the oven temperature to 140°C fan / 160°C / 325°F.

6 Once cooled, use a sharp knife to cut each rectangle into 2cm (¾in) slices. Place the slices flat on the baking tray and bake for a further 20–25 minutes until dry and golden. Allow to cool completely on a wire rack before gifting.

Gifting tip

- To gift, simply line a suitably sized metal tin with white baking parchment and neatly arrange the biscotti. See the gifting tips on page 93 for advice on using old metal tins for gluten-free gifts.

STAINED-GLASS
Tree Decoration Biscuits

D use a hard dairy-free alternative to butter

LL

F

VE follow the dairy-free advice and use 1 flax egg (see page 27) instead of the egg

V

Makes 20

Takes 35 minutes

• 200g (7oz) boiled sweets (candies)

For the biscuits

• 100g (½ cup minus 1 tbsp) butter, softened
• 100g (½ cup) caster (superfine) sugar
• 1 large egg, beaten
• 1½ tsp vanilla extract
• 1 tsp ground ginger
• 1 tsp ground cinnamon
• 270g (2 cups) gluten-free plain (all-purpose) flour, plus extra for dusting
• ½ tsp xanthan gum

Tip: To make chocolate festive-spiced biscuits, replace 20g (¾oz) of the flour with 20g (¾oz) unsweetened cocoa powder.

If someone made these for me, I'd be the happiest gluten-free gal in the world! Remember that the biscuits will start to soften when hung on the tree for more than 2–3 days, so it's best to enjoy them sooner rather than later. Also, please ensure that they're not hung on your tree alongside anything containing gluten or on a tree that has had gluten-containing biscuits (for example) hung on it before. I never thought I'd have to mention cross-contamination of Christmas trees, but there you go!

1 Separate the boiled sweets into groups of the same colour, transfer each group one at a time to a mixing bowl and crush (still in their wrappers) using the end of a rolling pin. Remove the wrappers and set aside.

2 Preheat the oven to 170°C fan / 190°C / 375°F. Line two large baking trays with non-stick baking parchment.

3 In a large mixing bowl, cream together the butter and sugar until light and fluffy – I use an electric hand whisk or a stand mixer. Add the beaten egg and vanilla extract and briefly mix. Next, add the spices, flour and xanthan gum. Mix until all the flour is combined and it comes together as a dough.

4 Lightly flour a large sheet of non-stick baking parchment (and a rolling pin) and roll out the dough to a 6mm (2⅓in) thickness. Cut out star shapes using a large star biscuit (cookie) cutter and make a hole using a straw where string can be threaded through to hang them.

5 Transfer the shapes to a prepared tray, ideally using a large palette knife, then use a smaller star cutter to cut out the middle of the star shapes. Remove the middles (transfer to the second tray) and fill the star-shaped holes with one colour of crushed boiled sweets – about 2 boiled sweets' worth should suffice per biscuit. Repeat for all the star shapes.

6 Place both trays in the oven and bake for 8–10 minutes until the edges are *very* slightly golden. Allow the cookies to cool on the trays for a few minutes before transferring to a wire rack to cool completely. The stained glass biscuits are the 'star' of the show here, but the middle cut-outs are just too good to waste. Either ice patterns on them using royal icing (page 58) or simply include when gifting along with the stained-glass biscuits.

CHOCOLATE MARSHMALLOW, SCHOOL DINNER JAM SPONGE, OR ANGEL CAKE

Cake Jars

 D use a hard dairy-free alternative to butter and dairy-free dark chocolate

 LL use lactose-free chocolate

 **F** use lactose-free chocolate

 V

Makes 4 cake jars

Takes 50 minutes

For the sponge base

- 225g (1 cup) butter, softened
- 225g (1 cup plus 2 tbsp) caster (superfine) sugar
- 4 eggs
- 225g (1¾ cups) gluten-free self-raising (self-rising) flour
- 1 tsp gluten-free baking powder
- ¼ tsp xanthan gum

For the chocolate marshmallow sponge

- 40g (1½oz) unsweetened cocoa powder (reduce the flour in the base by this amount)

For the chocolate icing and filling

- 110g (3¾oz) dark chocolate
- 250g (1 cup plus 2 tbsp) butter, softened
- 185g (1¼ cups) icing (confectioners') sugar
- 55g (½ cup) unsweetened cocoa powder
- 6-7 tbsp marshmallow fluff

For the school dinner sponge

- 1 tsp vanilla extract

In my mind, this is the ultimate gluten-free gift because not only is it a cake in a jar, but it's the type of thing we wish we could easily buy in supermarkets or safely online. Fortunately, making these is even easier than making cupcakes, and I've given you three variations to choose from, though you're of course welcome to come up with your own using the measurements provided too.

1 Preheat the oven to 160°C fan / 180°C / 350°F. Line a 12-hole cupcake tray with cupcake cases. I like to sprinkle a few grains of dried rice beneath each case, as it helps to absorb unwanted moisture.

2 In a large mixing bowl, cream together the butter and sugar until light and pale – I prefer to use an electric hand whisk or a stand mixer for this. Crack in the eggs, one at a time, mixing in between each addition until well combined. Sift in the flour, baking powder and xanthan gum, then fold in.

- If making the chocolate marshmallow sponge, remember to reduce the flour in the base and add sifted cocoa powder instead.
- If making the school dinner sponge, add the vanilla extract and stir in.
- If making the angel cake, separate the cake batter equally between 3 bowls. Add pink food colouring and raspberry extract to one, yellow food colouring and lemon extract to one and vanilla extract to the other before briefly folding in. The idea is to bake three variations of different flavoured/coloured cupcakes that we'll layer up later.

3 Spoon the mixture(s) evenly into the cupcake cases (I fill mine just over two-thirds full) and bake in the oven for 20–25 minutes until cooked through. To check, insert a skewer into the middle of one, and if it comes out clean, it's done! Allow the cupcakes to cool completely on a wire rack.

4 Now make the icing for your chosen variation of cake jar.

To make the chocolate icing

- First melt the dark chocolate (I do this in the microwave, mixing in between short bursts until melted), then put to one side and allow to cool slightly while you make the rest of the buttercream.

For the school dinner cake icing

- 400g (2¾ cups) icing (confectioners') sugar
- 1 tsp vanilla extract
- 4–6 tbsp gluten-free multi-coloured sprinkles

For the angel cake sponge

- Tiny drop of pink food colouring gel
- ½ tsp raspberry extract
- Tiny drop of yellow food colouring gel
- ½ tsp lemon extract
- ½ tsp vanilla extract

For the angel cake icing and filling

- 225g (1 cup) butter, softened
- 450g (3¼ cups) icing (confectioners') sugar
- 1 tsp vanilla extract
- 6–7 tbsp strawberry jam (jelly)

- Place the butter in the bowl of a stand mixer and mix on a medium speed for about 5 minutes until fluffy and paler. Add the icing sugar in 2 stages, beating for about 3 minutes between each addition. Start your mixer slowly to avoid creating a mini icing sugar explosion, but then increase the speed to medium-high for each of your 3-minute mixing intervals. Sift in the cocoa powder and then mix again until fully combined.

- Add the slightly cooled, melted chocolate and mix until fully incorporated. If the icing seems too thick, just add a teaspoon or so of milk (dairy-free if necessary) to loosen it up. Transfer to a piping (pastry) bag – no need for a nozzle – and when you're ready to use it, simply snip off a 1cm (½in) opening. Place the marshmallow fluff in a second piping bag and snip off a 1cm (½in) opening.

To make the school dinner sponge icing

- Sift the icing sugar into a large mixing bowl. Add the vanilla extract and very gradually add water a tablespoon at a time, mixing until it becomes the right consistency. It should be quite thick and glossy; don't let it go too runny (sift in more icing sugar if this happens).

To make the angel cake icing

- I use a stand mixer for this and the chocolate icing, but an electric hand whisk will do the job just fine too. If making by hand, ensure you mix for longer, until everything is well-combined and consistent.

- Place the butter in the bowl of a stand mixer and mix on a medium speed for about 5 minutes until the butter has turned a lot paler. Add the icing sugar in 2–3 stages, beating for about 3 minutes between each addition. Start your mixer slowly to avoid creating a mini icing sugar explosion, but then increase the speed to medium-high for each of your 3-minute mixing intervals. Add the vanilla extract and mix until fully combined. If the icing seems too thick, just add a teaspoon or so of milk (dairy-free if necessary) to loosen it up.

- Transfer to a piping (pastry) bag – no need for a nozzle – and when you're ready to use it, simply snip off a 1cm (½in) opening. Place the jam in a second piping bag and snip off a 5mm (¼in) opening.

To construct

5 Take a roughly 500ml (2 cup) jam jar and crumble one cupcake into the base, gently compacting it into a flat layer with the end of a wooden spoon.

6 If using a filling (marshmallow fluff or jam), pipe a thin layer of it on top, starting at the very edges of the jar and working your way in. For the chocolate marshmallow and angel cake jars, pipe a generous layer of icing next. For the school dinner jam sponge, simply use a spoon to generously drizzle in the icing around the edge of the glass and in the centre to create an even layer, then scatter with sprinkles.

7 Repeat the layers of cake and toppings until your jar is full (you'll need about 3 cupcakes per jar), then pop the lid on. For the angel cake jar, ensure you use a layer of all three varieties of cupcake in each jar. Repeat for the other three jars. Keep stored in a dry, cool place for 3–4 days.

Fudge

CHOCOLATE HAZELNUT, RASPBERRY AND WHITE CHOCOLATE CRUNCH OR MINT CHOCOLATE CRUNCH

V

Makes 36 squares

Takes 10 minutes
+ 4 hours chilling

- 1 x 397g (14oz) can of condensed milk

For chocolate hazelnut

- 250g (9oz) milk chocolate, broken into small chunks
- 100g (3½oz) dark chocolate, broken into small chunks
- 120g (4oz) blanched whole hazelnuts
- 30g (1oz) chopped roasted hazelnuts, plus 40g (1½oz) extra to scatter on top

For white chocolate and raspberry crunch

- 450g (16oz) white chocolate, broken into small chunks
- 6g (⅙oz) freeze-dried raspberries, plus 3g (¹⁄₁₀oz) to scatter on top
- 2 tsp raspberry extract
- Small drop of red food colouring gel
- 20g (¾oz) gluten-free rice crispy cereal

For mint chocolate crunch

- 350g (12oz) dark mint chocolate, broken into small chunks
- 30g (1oz) gluten-free rice crispy cereal
- 100g (3½oz) mint chocolate thins, roughly chopped, to scatter on top

Even though everyone will be impressed you made these yourself, fudge is a doddle to make and is the perfect gift for a crowd, especially as they can be easily gift wrapped in paper and tied with a ribbon individually. As supermarkets often stock freeze-dried raspberries and raspberry extract *or* freeze-dried strawberries and strawberry extract (not usually both), remember that either (or a combination of both) will work just fine.

1 Line a 20cm (8in) square baking tin (pan) with non-stick baking parchment.

2 To prepare the base in the microwave, place the condensed milk and chocolate of choice in a medium heatproof mixing bowl and place in the microwave on a low heat setting (I set mine to 180W in a 900W microwave) for 5–6 minutes, stirring halfway. Remove from the microwave and stir the mixture until all the chocolate is fully melted and smooth. Alternatively, place the ingredients in a large saucepan over a low heat until everything is melted and smooth, stirring occasionally.

3 Add in the whole and chopped hazelnuts, freeze-dried raspberries, raspberry extract, food colouring gel and rice crispy cereal, depending on which variation you're making. Stir in until evenly dispersed.

4 Pour the mixture into the prepared tin and smooth out into an even layer. Scatter on any toppings, like more chopped hazelnuts, freeze-dried raspberries or mint chocolate thins, and gently press in using a silicone spatula.

5 Place in the fridge to chill for 4–5 hours. Remove from the fridge, remove from the tin and peel off the baking parchment. Transfer to a chopping board and slice into 6 rows vertically and horizontally, using a sharp knife. Store in the fridge in a sealed container until ready to gift.

Freezable: Once cut into small pieces, freeze in an airtight container for up to 3 months.

Gifting tip

- Either wrap individual pieces of fudge in greaseproof paper and secure with string tied into a bow, or gift multiple pieces in old jam jars.

IRISH CREAM, WHITE CHOCOLATE SNOWBALL OR TIFFIN

Truffles

Makes 34–42

Takes 30 minutes
+ 4 hours chilling

Despite their neatly crafted appearance, truffles are very easy to make. Once you've thrown together the mixture and chilled it, all that's left to do is roll the set ganache into balls and coat to create the perfect gluten-free gift. Feel free to get creative with flavours! (Pictured on page 81.)

For Irish cream truffles

- 300g (10½oz) mixture of milk and dark chocolate, broken into small chunks
- 225ml (1 cup minus 1 tbsp) double (heavy) cream
- 2 tbsp butter
- 3 tbsp Irish cream liqueur
- 150g (5oz) milk chocolate, for coating

For white chocolate snowball truffles

- 350g (12oz) white chocolate, broken into small chunks
- 75ml (⅓ cup) double (heavy) cream
- 2 tbsp butter
- 60g (2oz) desiccated (dried shredded) coconut, for coating

For tiffin truffles

- 300g (10½oz) mixture of milk and dark chocolate, broken into small chunks
- 225ml (1 cup minus 1 tbsp) double (heavy) cream
- 2 tbsp butter
- 10 gluten-free digestive biscuits (graham crackers), crushed or blitzed to a rough powder
- 4 tbsp raisins, chopped

1 To prepare the ganache in the microwave, place the chocolate, cream and butter in a medium heatproof mixing bowl and place in the microwave on a low heat setting (I set mine to 180W in a 900W microwave) for 5 minutes, stirring halfway. Remove from the microwave and stir until all the chocolate is fully melted and smooth. The white chocolate mixture can look quite separated, but that's totally normal. Alternatively, prepare on the hob by placing the chocolate, cream and butter in a large saucepan over a low heat. Heat until everything is melted and smooth, stirring occasionally.

2 Stir in the Irish cream liqueur or half of the crushed digestive biscuits and all of the raisins, depending on which variation you are making. Allow to cool for 20 minutes, then cover and place in the fridge for 4 hours until firm.

3 Line a large baking tray with non-stick baking parchment. Use a teaspoon or melon baller to take equal portions of the ganache and transfer to the baking tray until all the ganache is used up. Place the baking tray back in the fridge for 15 minutes, to ensure they are not too soft and sticky when you roll them into balls. If making the white chocolate truffles, you can likely skip this step as it should be firm enough already.

4 If making the Irish cream truffles, melt the milk chocolate in a small bowl in a microwave (180W for 4 minutes, stirring twice or in a heatproof bowl set over a half-filled saucepan of boiling water). For the other variations grab a large dinner plate and spread out either the desiccated coconut or remaining blitzed biscuits.

5 Remove the ganache portions from the fridge and roll into balls using your hands. Next, roll in the desiccated coconut or crushed biscuits, or impale with a cocktail stick and dip into the melted chocolate, depending on which variation you're making. Transfer back to the lined baking tray, then return the tray to the fridge until set. Transfer to truffle paper cases and arrange in paper food boxes ready for gifting, both of which you can buy online.

Tip: Rolling the balls in your hands can get messy if the ganache isn't cold enough, so always ensure it is well set before rolling! For the same reason, the finished truffles must always be kept chilled, otherwise they can become very soft; make sure your giftee is aware of this.

Freezable: Once coated, freeze in an airtight container for up to 3 months.

Macarons

 D use a hard dairy-free butter alternative and dairy-free milk, if needed

 LL use lactose-free milk, if needed

 F use lactose-free milk, if needed

V

Makes 16

Takes 50 minutes
+ cooling/resting time

For the macarons

- 100g (¾ cup) icing (confectioners') sugar
- 100g (1 cup) ground almonds
- 2 large egg whites (about 35g/1¼oz each)
- ½ tsp strawberry or vanilla extract
- Food colouring gel of your choice
- 100g (½ cup) caster (superfine) sugar
- 30ml (2 tbsp) water

For the buttercream

- 75g (⅓ cup) butter, softened
- 150g (1¼ cups) icing (confectioners') sugar
- 1 tsp strawberry or vanilla extract
- Food colouring gel of your choice
- 1–2 tsp milk (optional)

Freezable: Once constructed, freeze in an airtight container for up to 1 month

I'll never forget walking into a certain (very famous) Parisian bakery and being surrounded by a sea of macarons; not only because of the vibrant colours, but because they were all gluten-free! So do as I do and give a little Parisian gluten-free magic this Christmas, conjured up right in your own kitchen.

1 Prepare two large baking trays lined with non-stick baking parchment. You can optionally draw 4cm (2in) circles in pencil on the parchment with a 2cm (1in) gap between each circle, then flip it over – this helps to guide your piping.

2 Blitz the icing sugar and ground almonds in a food processor, then sift the mixture into a large mixing bowl to remove any larger lumps, which can then be discarded.

3 Separate the egg whites into two separate bowls and add one of the egg whites to the almond and sugar bowl along with the strawberry or vanilla extract. Mix to combine until it forms a paste. Stir in a few drops of food colouring gel; make the mixture a little brighter than you're aiming for, as it will become less bright when you add the remaining ingredients. Cover the bowl and set aside.

4 Place the caster sugar and water in a small saucepan and set over a low–medium heat. At the same time, place the other egg white into the bowl of a stand mixer with a whisk attachment. Once the sugar syrup has reached 110°C (230°F) – I use a digital food thermometer for this part - turn the mixer to a medium speed and whisk the egg white until you achieve soft peaks.

5 Once the sugar syrup gets to 118°C (245°F), remove it from the heat and slowly pour it straight into the stand mixer bowl in a thin stream while the mixer is still running. Once you've added all the sugar syrup, turn the speed up to high and whisk for 5-10 minutes until cooler. You should have a glossy meringue mixture that isn't too stiff.

6 Add a little of the meringue mixture to the almond paste and fold it in using a silicone spatula. Then gradually fold the rest of the meringue mixture in until the mixture is smooth and has a slight shine. Do this carefully so that you don't knock the air out - it's important not to overmix. When ready, the mixture should form ribbons when drizzled from the spatula that disappear back into the mixture within 10 seconds.

Continued...

Tip: To clean the saucepan you made your sugar syrup in, simply fill with boiling water. Add in any utensils used too. Bring it to a simmer for 5-10 minutes and all the sugar will magically dissolve into the water. If you use cold water to clean your pan, the sugar syrup will harden and be near impossible to remove!

7 Now it's time to pipe the mixture. Place the mixture into a piping (pastry) bag fitted with a 1cm (½in) round piping tip and pipe 4cm (2in) circles onto the paper, leaving a 2cm (1in) gap between each. When piping, keep the piping bag completely vertical to the paper and pipe from the centre at all times. Quickly flick out sideways to finish piping, which will prevent peaks forming. Once you've used up all the mixture, tap the trays firmly on the work surface a few times and then put to one side for about 40 minutes to dry out and form a skin. They're ready when you can gently touch the tops and there's no residue left on your finger.

8 Preheat the oven to 140°C fan / 160°C / 325°F.

9 Bake the macarons for about 18 minutes, or until they've risen up slightly and have visible 'feet' – a new bottom layer that wasn't there before baking. Remove from the oven and allow to fully cool on the tray.

10 While they're cooling, make the buttercream filling. Place the softened butter into the (cleaned) bowl of a stand mixer (or a large mixing bowl if using an electric hand mixer). Mix on a medium speed for around 6 minutes, until the butter has turned paler in colour. Add the icing sugar in 2 stages, beating for about 3 minutes between each addition. Start the mixer slowly to avoid creating a mini icing sugar explosion, but then increase the speed to medium-high for each of your 3-minute mixing intervals. Add the strawberry or vanilla extract as well as the gel food colouring and mix until fully combined. If the buttercream is too thick, loosen with a little milk, 1 teaspoon at a time, until you're happy with the consistency. Transfer to a piping bag fitted with a ½cm (¼in) round nozzle.

11 Pipe the buttercream onto the underside of one of the cooled macaron halves, starting at the edges and working towards the middle in a circular motion. The buttercream should be no more than ½cm (¼in) thick. Sandwich another macaron half on top. Repeat until you've used up all of the macaron halves and/or buttercream. Chill briefly in the fridge and then package ready for gifting.

Gifting tip

- You can buy macaron boxes online which are perfect for presenting your wondrous creations and wrapping up ready for gifting.

Lemon Amaretti Biscuits

D · LF · F · V

Makes 25

Takes 30 minutes

- 2 large or medium egg whites
- 170g (¾ cup plus 1½ tbsp) caster (superfine) sugar
- 170g (1¾ cups) ground almonds
- 1 tbsp lemon juice or limoncello
- Grated zest of 2 lemons

For rolling

- 3 tbsp caster (superfine) sugar
- 3 tbsp icing (confectioners') sugar

Freezable: Once cooled, freeze in an airtight container for up to 3 months.

To me, lemon and almonds immediately taste like a lemon Bakewell, so if that sounds up your street (or up that of the person lucky enough to receive this), then you've come to the right place. These meringue-like Italian biscuits are sweet, crunchy on the outside and yet sticky and chewy in the middle and make the perfect gift for, well… everyone.

1 Preheat the oven to 160°C fan / 180°C / 350°F. Lightly grease a baking tray and line with non-stick baking parchment.

2 In a large mixing bowl, beat the egg whites using an electric hand whisk until fluffy and medium peaks form. Next, add the sugar, ground almonds, lemon juice/limoncello and lemon zest, then fold in using a silicone spatula to form a wet dough.

3 Grab two side plates and spread out the caster sugar on one and the icing sugar on the other.

4 Take a heaped teaspoon of the mixture, roll into a ball in your hands and then roll on the caster sugar plate, followed by the icing sugar plate. Place slightly spaced out on the prepared baking tray.

5 Bake for 15–20 minutes or until slightly cracked and golden beneath the sugar. Allow to fully cool on the tray.

Gifting tip

- These biscuits are perfect to gift in jars, finishing with a little ribbon fashioned into a bow. Old glass coffee jars work perfectly as they tend to be a little bigger than jam jars – I find removing the labels to be quite easy after they've had a full cycle in the dishwasher.

Cheeseboard Biscuits

D — use a hard dairy-free alternative to butter and dairy-free cheese

LL

F

VE — see dairy-free advice

V — use a veggie-friendly grana padano instead of parmesan, if using

Serves 6–8

Takes 20 minutes
+ 45 minutes chilling time
+ 12 minutes baking time

For the crackers

- 225g (1¾ cups) gluten-free plain (all-purpose) flour, plus extra for dusting
- ½ tsp xanthan gum
- 1½ tsp gluten-free baking powder
- 90g (⅓ cup plus 1 tbsp) cold butter, cubed
- ½ tsp salt
- ½ tsp caster (superfine) sugar
- 30ml (2 tbsp) extra virgin olive oil
- 40ml (2 tbsp plus 2 tsp) cold water

For rosemary and parmesan

- 2 tsp dried rosemary
- 50g (1¾oz) parmesan, grated

For paprika and cheddar

- 1 tsp smoked paprika
- 60g (2oz) Cheddar, grated

For mixed seed

- 1–2 tbsp mixed seeds (pumpkin, sesame, sunflower)

To finish

- 25g (scant 2 tbsp) butter, melted
- Flaky salt, for sprinkling

I've been to many festive celebrations over the years where a cheeseboard has been produced and I've ended up 'enjoying' cheese without the biscuits because little ol' gluten-free me wasn't thought about. Don't get me wrong, I love cheese, but biscuits or crackers are definitely a necessary facilitator! Gluten-free biscuits for cheese are widely available in supermarkets these days but there's nothing like homemade, especially as you can switch up the flavour combos.

1 Mix together the flour, xanthan gum and baking powder in a large mixing bowl. Add the cubed butter and rub it in with your fingertips until you achieve a breadcrumb-like consistency – you could also use a food processor for this part to speed things up a bit.

2 Stir in the salt, sugar and the additional flavourings of your choice, depending on which variation you are making, then add the oil, followed by the water, cutting it in with a knife so it gradually starts to come together. Use your hands to bring the mixture together into a ball, wrap in cling film (plastic wrap), then place in the fridge to chill for 45 minutes.

3 Preheat the oven to 160°C fan / 180°C / 350°F. Line a baking tray with non-stick baking parchment.

4 On a lightly floured piece of non-stick baking parchment, roll out the dough to a 4mm (⅛in) thickness and use either a round, rectangular or square cutter (or cut shapes with a knife) to make biscuit (cookie) shapes. Re-roll the dough as necessary to cut out as many shapes as possible.

5 Transfer the shapes to the prepared tray, ideally using a small palette knife, then prick a few holes in each of them using a fork. Bake for about 12–14 minutes until golden. Remove from the oven, brush with melted butter and sprinkle with some flaky salt. Allow to fully cool on the baking tray.

Freezable: Once cooled, freeze in an airtight container for up to 3 months.

Gifting tip

- To gift, simply line a suitably sized metal tin with white baking parchment and arrange the biscuits by flavour. See the gifting tips on page 93 for advice on using old metal tins for gluten-free gifts.

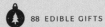

Sticky Tomato Chutney

D LF F VE V

65g (2¼oz) is a safe low
FODMAP serving size

Makes 2 x 350ml
(1½ cup) jars

Takes 1 hour

- 2 large leeks (green parts only),
  thinly sliced (200-250g/7-9oz
  once chopped)
- 1kg (2lb 3oz) tomatoes,
  chopped
- 300g (1½ cups) light brown
  sugar
- 300ml (1¼ cups) red wine
  vinegar
- 1 tsp dried chilli flakes
- 1 tsp salt

As someone in the maintenance phase of the low FODMAP diet, this is probably the best gift I could possibly receive. Commonly, chutney is made with both apples and onion, which are in too great a quantity to be safe for the elimination phase of the diet, especially when combined with a boatload of tomatoes too. However, this chutney is elimination phase safe and you'd never even know! If you have no idea what the low FODMAP diet even is, then feel free to head over to page 33 to read more about it. (Pictured on page 89.)

1 Add all the ingredients to a large saucepan and bring to the boil over a medium heat. Simmer for 40-50 minutes or until all of the tomatoes are softened.

2 Turn the heat up to high and reduce the mixture down, stirring occasionally until it starts to become sticky. At this point, stir more regularly and continue until it comes together, thickens and becomes more jammy.

3 Portion into sterilized jars and allow to cool completely before popping on the lids and storing in the fridge. Keep chilled and use within 1 month, or store unopened in the fridge for up to 3 months.

Freezable: Once cooled, freeze in an airtight container for up to 12 months.

Gifting tips

- Get creative creating your own labels for the jars, ready for gifting. Everyone loves personalised gifts so something like 'Mark's low FODMAP chutney' would be a good start!

- Bonus points if you create an extra label on the back with an ingredients list so your giftee can feel confident knowing what's in it.

Bearded Rudolf Chocolate Bark (WITH POPPING CANDY)

D — use dairy-free chocolate and omit the popping candy

LF — use lactose-free chocolate and omit the popping candy

F — see lactose-free advice

VE — see dairy-free advice

V

Makes 1 large slab

Takes 10 minutes
+ 2 hours chilling

- 150g (5oz) milk chocolate, broken into small chunks
- 150g (5oz) dark chocolate, broken into small chunks
- 3 tbsp popping candy
- 75g (2½oz) white chocolate, broken into small chunks
- 5 small round red sweets (candies) or chocolates (ensure gluten-free)
- 10 edible eyes (ensure gluten-free)
- 10 small gluten-free pretzels
- Small handful of red, green and white gluten-free festive sprinkles

What screams Christmas more than chocolate Rudolf bark (complete with a white chocolate Santa beard), laced with popping candy and festive sprinkles? Once set, simply smash into shards, wrap in festive wax paper and gift. You should be able to find small bags of gluten-free pretzels down supermarket gluten-free or 'free from' aisles – you'll need these for Rudolf's antlers.

1 Loosely line a 33 x 25cm (13 x 10in) baking tray with non-stick baking parchment.

2 Place the milk and dark chocolate in a small heatproof bowl. Microwave on a low setting (180W in a 900W microwave) for 4–5 minutes, stirring halfway, and again once it emerges. Alternatively, melt the chocolate in a heatproof bowl set over a half-filled saucepan of boiling water. Stir the popping candy through the melted milk/dark chocolate. Melt the white chocolate in the same way in a separate bowl; if microwaving, set to 180W again but only for 2–3 minutes.

3 Pour the melted milk/dark chocolate onto the lined tray and spread out using a silicone spatula – no need to spread it right up to the edges. Use a teaspoon to dollop the white chocolate on top (nicely spaced apart, leaving some space above each) then use a skewer or chopstick to drag out and swirl each white dollop into a beard shape.

4 Place the red sweets or chocolates just above the white chocolate swirly beard, then the two eyes above that and finally, two pretzels as antlers. Repeat for all the other white chocolate beards. Lastly, scatter red, green and white sprinkles in any spaces. Place in the fridge for 2–3 hours to set.

5 To smash into neat pieces, simply lift the slab off the baking parchment a little and confidently tap where you want it to break – preferably around the Rudolfs!

CHOCOLATE BAR
Florentines

D

use a hard dairy-free alternative to butter and dairy-free chocolate

LL

use lactose-free chocolate

F

use maple syrup instead of golden syrup or honey and use lactose-free chocolate; one florentine is a safe low FODMAP serving size

VE

see dairy-free advice and use golden syrup instead of honey

V

Makes 15–17

Takes 25 minutes + cooling

- 50g (3½ tbsp) butter
- 50g (¼ cup) light brown sugar
- 50g (2 tbsp) golden syrup or honey
- 50g (6 tbsp) gluten-free plain (all-purpose) flour
- 200g (7oz) milk or dark chocolate, chopped into small pieces

For chocolate hazelnut florentines

- 85g (3oz) blanched hazelnuts, roughly chopped
- 35g (1¼oz) gluten-free cornflakes
- 2 tbsp chopped roasted hazelnuts

For picnic florentines

- 85g (3oz) roasted peanuts, chopped
- 35g (1¼oz) gluten-free rice crispy cereal
- 60g (2oz) raisins

These little festive treats are (usually) naturally gluten-free, in case you didn't know already! So to make this an extra-special gift for a gluten-free person, I've created three variations that are inspired by chocolate bars that are most definitely NOT gluten-free: a Kinder Bueno, a Picnic Bar and a Cadbury Fruit and Nut bar. Note that the chopped roasted hazelnuts come pre-chopped, but for the rest it's best to chop them yourself so there's a nice variation of textures in there.

1 Preheat the oven to 160°C fan / 180°C / 350°F. Line three baking trays with non-stick baking parchment.

2 Add the butter, sugar and syrup or honey to a large saucepan. Place over a low–medium heat until the butter is melted, then stir until smooth and consistent.

3 Stir in the flour until no lumps remain, then add the variation ingredients of your choice (the nuts, dried fruit and/or cereal). Stir in until well coated.

4 Take a heaped teaspoon of the mixture and use a second teaspoon to push it onto a lined baking tray. Ensure to leave a generous amount of space between the dollops for them to spread. Repeat until all of the mixture has been used up.

5 Place all the trays in the oven and bake for about 8 minutes, or until each of the dollops has spread to the size of a digestive biscuit (medium cookie).

6 Remove the trays from the oven and immediately use an 8cm (3in) biscuit (cookie) cutter to gently round each Florentine into a perfect circle, or to simply cut away the edges if they've spread too much. Allow to cool on the tray until you can pick them up without them bending – this should take around 15 minutes.

For fruit and nut florentines

- 75g (2½oz) blanched almonds, roughly chopped
- 20g (¾oz) roasted peanuts, roughly chopped
- 2 tbsp chopped roasted hazelnuts
- 25g (1oz) dried cranberries, roughly chopped
- 50g (1¾oz) raisins

7 Place the chocolate in a microwaveable bowl and microwave on full-power (900W) for 90 seconds, stirring every 20 seconds. Alternatively, melt the chocolate in a heatproof bowl set over a saucepan of boiling water (don't allow the bowl to touch the water), stirring until melted.

8 Take a tablespoon of melted chocolate and dollop it onto the back of a florentine, then quickly spread as close to the edges as you can using the back of the spoon. Place the florentine chocolate-side down back onto the non-stick baking parchment and gently press down and rotate back and forth until you can see the chocolate ooze out from all sides. Repeat with all of the florentines, then allow to set for about 1 hour.

Freezable: Once set, freeze in an airtight container for up to 3 months.

Gifting tips

- These are ideal for gifting in old metal tins (ensure they've been thoroughly cleaned first if they used to contain gluten; using tins with clear branding of gluten-containing products is probably best avoided so as not to give someone a fright!) lined with coloured tissue paper.

- A large glass jar would work well too, providing that the neck is wide enough to get them out easily.

- Be sure not to touch the chocolate too much when handling and packing them away, as it melts quite quickly, and clear fingerprints can easily be left. Store out of direct sunlight and away from radiators or any other heat source!

Festive Party Food

Cheat's Char Siu Pork Bao Buns

 D use dairy-free milk

 LF use lactose-free milk

 F use lactose-free milk

Makes 16

Takes 40 minutes + at least 2 hours marinating

- 700g (1½lb) pork shoulder steaks
- Handful of spring onion (scallion) greens, thinly sliced
- 1 medium red chilli, thinly sliced

For the marinade

- 1½ tsp Chinese five-spice powder
- 1 tsp cornflour (cornstarch)
- 5 tbsp dark brown sugar
- 2 tbsp garlic-infused oil
- 1 tsp red miso paste (ensure gluten-free)
- 4 tbsp gluten-free soy sauce
- 2 tbsp red wine vinegar
- 1 tbsp dry sherry or mirin
- Small drop of red food colouring gel (optional)

For the bao buns

- 330g (2½ cups) gluten-free self-raising (self-rising) flour
- 2 tsp caster (superfine) sugar
- 1 tsp salt
- 500ml (2 cups plus 1 tbsp) milk
- 2 large egg whites

This has always been Mark's favourite thing to eat when visiting his family in Malaysia, so it's not surprising he's made a gluten-free version that tastes *exactly* like the real deal. His super-fluffy steamed pancakes are the perfect cheat's bao bun, plus don't require proving or a bamboo steamer!

1 Place the pork steaks in a roasting dish. In a small bowl, mix the marinade ingredients until well combined, add to the pork steaks and ensure each steak is well coated. Cover and place in the fridge for 2–24 hours.

2 To cook the pork, preheat the oven to 200°C fan / 220°C / 425°F. Line a grill (broiler) pan with foil, then place the wire grill rack on top. Place the marinated steaks on the wire rack and roast for 25 minutes. Remove from the oven and brush with any leftover marinade. Flip the steaks over and brush the other side too, then return to the oven for 15 minutes. Allow to rest for 10 minutes before slicing thinly with a sharp knife. Cover and keep warm.

3 Meanwhile, make the bao buns. Place a large frying pan that has a lid over a very low heat. Prepare a small bowl of water and cut out sixteen 12.5cm (5in) squares of non-stick baking parchment; set aside.

4 In a large mixing bowl, combine the flour, sugar and salt. Add a third of the milk, whisk until smooth, then whisk in the remaining milk in two batches.

5 In a small bowl, whisk the egg whites to soft peaks – I use an electric hand whisk. Fold the whisked egg white into the bao batter using a spatula until no fluffy lumps remain. The mixture should be thickened but cloud-like.

6 Place 2 parchment squares in the frying pan. Dollop 3 tablespoons of bao bun mixture on top of each, then add 2 teaspoons of water to the very edge of the pan (ideally not touching the paper) – it should gently sizzle. Pop the lid on and steam for 4–5 minutes until the underside has a wavy light golden pattern and the middle of the top isn't sticky to the touch. Remove from the pan and, after 30 seconds, carefully peel off the parchment. Transfer to a plate for later and repeat until you've used up all of your bao batter.

7 To construct, take a bao bun and, with the golden side facing down, place the sliced pork on the top half. Sprinkle with spring onion greens, fold shut and top with 1–2 slices of fresh chilli.

Freezable: Once cooled, freeze the pork and bao buns in separate airtight containers for up to 1–2 months

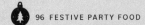

Not-Prawn Toast

Makes 56-64

Takes 25 minutes

- 14-16 small slices of white gluten-free bread (basically an entire loaf, assuming the loaf is small)
- 100g (¾ cup) sesame seeds
- 150ml (⅔ cup) vegetable oil

For the topping

- 250g (9oz) minced (ground) pork or chicken
- 1 tsp minced ginger paste
- 1 tbsp gluten-free soy sauce
- 1 tsp cornflour (cornstarch)
- 1 tsp sesame oil
- 2 tsp finely chopped chives
- ¼ tsp caster (superfine) sugar
- ¼ tsp ground black pepper
- 2 tbsp water
- 1 egg
- Pinch of salt

Freezable: Once cooled, freeze in an airtight container for up to 3 months.

For those of you who aren't into seafood, I have to inform you that you've been massively missing out on crispy, golden sesame prawn toast. However, if that simple statement doesn't alter your aversion to prawns, here's an alternative that uses pork or chicken mince to create something equally as mind-blowing, but totally different. It's a dim-sum-style filling crossed with a Chinese takeaway classic that'll please absolutely anyone. (Pictured on page 97.)

1 Preheat the oven to 200°C fan / 220°C / 425°F.

2 Add all the topping ingredients to a large mixing bowl and mix well until you have a smooth paste.

3 Spread the mixture generously (so you can't see the bread through the filling) across each slice of bread, making sure you go right up to the edges.

4 Pour the sesame seeds onto a large plate and spread them out evenly. Place the bread topping-side down in the sesame seeds until fully covered, then cut each topped slice of bread into 4 triangles.

5 Pour the vegetable oil into a small bowl. Dip each triangle into the oil until fully submerged, then place them all on a baking tray.

6 Bake in the oven for 10 minutes, flipping them halfway, until lightly golden brown.

To cook in the air fryer

- Preheat the air fryer to 200°C / 425°F. Place the triangles in the air fryer for 5-6 minutes until golden and crispy.

7 Serve with your favourite gluten-free sweet chilli dipping sauce.

VEG-ENDARY
Sausage Rolls

 **D** use a smoked dairy-free cheese

 LL

V

 VE use a smoked dairy-free cheese, use 50ml (3½ tbsp) almond milk in the filling instead of the egg, and brush with sweetened almond milk instead of egg

Makes 16 mini sausage rolls

Takes 30 minutes

- Vegetable oil, for greasing
- 1 x 280g (10oz) store-bought gluten-free puff pastry sheet
- 4 tsp wholegrain mustard
- 1 egg, beaten
- 3 tbsp poppy seeds
- Chutney (see page 90 for homemade) or tomato relish, to serve

For the filling

- 150g (5oz) chestnut (cremini) mushrooms, finely chopped
- 2 tbsp garlic-infused oil
- 3 tsp finely chopped fresh chives
- 1 tsp dried thyme
- 75g (2½oz) extra-mature Cheddar, grated
- 75g (2½oz) gluten-free breadcrumbs
- 50g (1¾oz) cooked and peeled chestnuts, finely chopped
- 1 medium egg

Freezable: Once cooled, freeze in an airtight container for up to 3 months.

What earns these crispy, golden beauties their 'legendary' title? It's simple – because these will be enjoyed by gluten eaters, meat eaters and gluten-free folks alike! With a gooey middle packed with tangy mustard, herbs and succulent chunks of mushroom, these will disappear when plated up – don't forget, you can double the filling and make a ton more using an extra sheet of gluten-free puff pastry.

1 Preheat the oven to 200°C fan / 220°C / 425°F, grease a large baking tray and line with non-stick baking parchment.

2 Put all the ingredients for the filling in a large mixing bowl and give it a good mix so it's all nicely dispersed.

3 Unroll the pastry on a flat work surface with a long side closest to you. Use a pizza cutter (I also use a ruler to ensure I'm cutting straight) to cut in half horizontally, dividing the pastry into two long strips. Spread the mustard in a long line along the strips, leaving about 1.25cm (½in) of clear space on the bottom edge and a larger space above the mustard.

4 Spoon the filling onto each pastry strip in a long line on top of the mustard, then compact it a little with your fingers so it's not so loose. Brush the narrower clear length of pastry with beaten egg and fold the other side of pastry over the filling to meet. Using your fingers, gently form the pastry around the filling, while compacting it to remove any gaps.

5 Crimp the pastry seam all along using a fork, to securely seal it shut. Use a large, sharp knife to cut into 4cm (1½in) mini sausage rolls, then transfer them to the prepared baking tray. Brush each sausage roll with beaten egg and sprinkle with poppy seeds.

6 Bake in the oven for 15 minutes or until the pastry is golden, then cover loosely with foil and cook for a further 5–7 minutes. Remove from the oven and place the sausage rolls on a wire rack to cool for 10 minutes.

To cook in the air fryer

- Preheat the air fryer to 200°C / 425°F and spray a little oil into the tray. Place as many sausage rolls as will fit in the basket without touching and cook for 10 minutes.

7 Serve with chutney or relish as a dip, and enjoy hot or cold.

Mini Cheesy Chicken Kyivs

 D use a hard dairy-free smoked cheese instead of blue or Gourney cheese

 LL use mozzarella instead of blue or Gourney cheese

 F use mozzarella instead of blue or Gourney cheese

Makes 11–12

Takes 30 minutes

- 100g (3½oz) creamy blue cheese or Gournay cheese (I use Boursin)
- Vegetable oil, for greasing
- 500g (1lb 2oz) minced (ground) chicken or turkey breast
- ½ tsp salt
- ¼ tsp ground black pepper
- 1 tsp lemon juice
- 1 tbsp gluten-free plain (all-purpose) flour
- 1 tbsp garlic-infused oil

For the coating

- 3 tbsp gluten-free plain (all-purpose) flour
- 2 eggs
- 8 tbsp gluten-free breadcrumbs

Freezable: Once cooled, freeze in an airtight container for up to 3 months.

These little bites of garlicky joy are crispy on the outside with a melted cheesy middle. I've added timings for the oven and the air fryer as they turn out great in both, though the air fryer is a little faster.

1 Preheat the oven to 180°C fan / 200°C / 400°F.

2 Cut the cheese into 1.5cm (⅔in) cubes and keep chilled ready for later. Lightly grease a large baking tray with vegetable oil.

3 Add the minced chicken or turkey, salt, pepper, lemon juice, flour and oil to a large mixing bowl and mix well using a wooden spoon until combined and the mixture is more like a smooth paste.

4 Spread the flour for the coating out on a small plate. Grab two small bowls and crack the eggs into one, beat with a fork, and add the breadcrumbs to the other bowl.

5 Use an ice-cream scoop to take a portion of the mince mixture, then compact it against the side of the bowl. Turn each portion out onto a plate so they're ready to shape.

6 To construct the mini Kyivs, take a portion of the mince and roll it into a ball. Poke a hole into the middle with your finger and add a cube of cheese, right into the middle. Form the mince around the cube of cheese, then re-roll into a ball, making sure the cheese has an even layer of mince around it – this will ensure minimal leakage.

7 Next, roll the ball on the flour plate until lightly dusted, then dredge in the egg bowl until fully coated, and then roll in the breadcrumbs until there are no gaps in the coating. Place on the prepared baking tray. Repeat until you've used up all the mince.

8 Bake in the oven for 15 minutes, turning the balls over halfway through.

To cook in the air fryer

- Preheat the air fryer to 180°C / 350°F. Place the balls in the air fryer for 10 minutes, turning them over halfway.

9 Serve with tomato ketchup as a dip.

Mini Pizzas

D — use a thick dairy-free yoghurt and dairy-free cheese

LL — use lactose-free Greek yoghurt

F — use lactose-free yoghurt and use FODMAP-friendly toppings

VE — see dairy-free advice and use vegan-friendly toppings

V — use veggie-friendly toppings

Makes 12 x 7.5cm (3in) mini pizzas

Takes 30 minutes

- 200g (1½ cups) gluten-free self-raising (self-rising) flour, plus extra for dusting
- 115g (½ cup) Greek yoghurt or any thick plain yoghurt (give it a good stir before using)
- 2 tsp dried Italian herbs
- 50ml (3½ tbsp) water
- 60ml (¼ cup) passata (sieved tomatoes)
- 1 tsp garlic-infused oil
- 4–5 fresh basil leaves, finely chopped
- Pinch each of salt and ground black pepper
- 125g (4½oz) mozzarella, thinly sliced
- Extra toppings of your choice (such as pepperoni, ham and pineapple, tuna or roasted peppers)

Tip: If using a different type of yoghurt that isn't quite as thick, simply add a little more flour to compensate.

Freezable: Once cooled, freeze in an airtight container for up to 3 months.

Unfortunately, the only time you get novelty-sized food when you're gluten-free is when you *don't* want it – like when buying a loaf of bread. Fortunately, this is the type of novelty-sized food we do want, as any Christmas party food buffet wouldn't be complete without pizza! Feel free to top with whatever you like, whether it be canned tuna (very Italian), ham and pineapple (definitely not Italian) or whatever else you like!

1 Preheat the oven to 240°C fan / 260°C / 500°F, or as hot as your oven will go.

2 Add the flour, yoghurt, dried herbs and water to a large mixing bowl and mix thoroughly using a spatula to ensure there's no hidden clumps of yoghurt-coated flour. Use your hands to bring it together into a slightly sticky ball.

3 Knead the dough briefly in the bowl until smooth, combined and no longer sticky. Dough still too sticky? Add a little more flour to the dough. Dough too dry? Add a little more yoghurt.

4 Transfer the dough to a large sheet of lightly floured non-stick baking parchment. Lightly flour the rolling pin and roll out the dough to a large rectangle, aiming for an even 1mm (⅟₁₆in) thickness. Re-flour the rolling pin as necessary to stop it sticking.

5 Use a 7.5cm (3in) plain round cookie cutter to cut out as many circles from the dough as possible. Ensure they're close together so as little as possible is wasted, then peel away the excess dough, leaving only the circles.

6 Use the baking parchment to lift the dough circles onto a large baking tray. Form the discarded dough into a ball, then re-roll on a second sheet of baking parchment, cutting circles out of it once again. Lift onto a smaller baking tray.

7 In a bowl, mix the passata, oil, basil and seasoning, then dollop ½ teaspoon of the sauce onto each pizza. Use the back of the spoon to spread it to the edges.

8 Lay a thin slice of mozzarella on top of each mini pizza (and add any other toppings of your choice), then bake in the hot oven for 10–12 minutes or until the cheese is nicely browned and golden.

BUTTERNUT SQUASH AND SAGE
Baked Arancini

use dairy-free cream cheese and a smoked dairy-free cheese instead of grana Padano

use lactose-free cream cheese

use leek (green parts only) instead of onion, low FODMAP vegetable stock and lactose-free cream cheese; one arancini ball is a safe low FODMAP serving size

VE

follow the dairy-free advice, then use 150ml (⅔ cup) dairy-free milk to coat the floured balls instead of the eggs

ensure grana Padano is veggie-friendly

Makes 30

Takes 60–80 minutes + cooling

For the risotto base

- 1 medium butternut squash (800g/1½lb prepared weight), peeled, deseeded and cut into bite-sized chunks
- 5 tbsp garlic-infused oil, plus extra for greasing
- 2 tbsp butter
- ½ leek or 1 onion, finely chopped
- 300g (10½oz) risotto rice
- 1 litre (generous 4 cups) boiling water, mixed with 1 gluten-free vegetable stock cube
- Handful of fresh sage leaves, finely chopped
- 1 tsp salt
- ½ tsp ground black pepper
- 2 tbsp cream cheese
- 3 tbsp grated grana Padano

For the arancini

- 8–10 tbsp gluten-free plain (all-purpose) flour
- 3 large eggs
- 170g (6oz) gluten-free breadcrumbs (store-bought)

Freezable: Once cooled, freeze in an airtight container for up to 3 months.

What if I told you that you could make super-crispy arancini balls without the need to deep fry? Once you've made the risotto, allow it to cool, coat well and then simply bake or air fry to perfection - the choice is yours.

1 Place the butternut squash in a mixing bowl with 2 tablespoons of the garlic-infused oil and mix well. To roast in the oven, spread out on a baking tray and bake for 25 minutes or until browned at the edges, turning over halfway. To air fry, place in the air fryer basket for 15 minutes, turning halfway.

2 Meanwhile, place a large frying pan that has a lid over a medium heat, then add the remaining 3 tablespoons of garlic-infused oil and the butter. Once the butter has melted, add the leek/onion and fry for 3–4 minutes until softened, before adding the rice. Stir for 2 minutes until well coated in the fats, then add the stock, sage, salt and pepper. Briefly stir. Cover and cook on a low heat for 10 minutes, then remove the lid and simmer, stirring occasionally for a further 10 minutes or so. Once the rice is cooked, add the cream cheese and grana Padano and stir in until the risotto is thick and creamy. Lastly, stir in the roasted butternut squash. Allow to cool completely.

3 Preheat the oven 200°C fan / 220°C / 425°F. Lightly grease two large (clean) baking trays with oil. Spread the flour out onto a large dinner plate. Crack the eggs into a small bowl and briefly beat with a fork. Spread the breadcrumbs out onto a second large dinner plate.

4 Use an ice-cream scoop to take a heaped portion of the cooled risotto and compact it really well using the palm of your hand. Roll it into a ball then place on a board or plate. Repeat until you have used up all the risotto.

5 Take a risotto ball and roll it on the plate of flour until well coated, then in the egg bowl, then in the breadcrumbs. Place on the prepared trays and repeat until all of your arancini balls are coated. Spray the balls well with oil.

6 Bake in the oven for 15 minutes until golden and crispy.

To cook in the air fryer

- Preheat the air fryer to 200°C / 400°F and spray the base with oil. Place the balls in the air fryer, evenly spaced apart, and cook for 5–6 minutes until golden and crisp.

PORK, APPLE AND SAGE
Sausage Roll Wreath

D   **LL**   **F** replace the apple sauce with 1 large egg

Serves 10

Takes 45 minutes

- 1 quantity of gluten-free ultimate shortcrust pastry (page 204)
- 5 tbsp wholegrain mustard
- 1 egg, beaten
- Handful of poppy seeds
- Cranberry sauce, to serve

For the sausagemeat filling

- 500g (1lb 2oz) minced (ground) pork
- 2 slices of white gluten-free bread, blitzed in a food processor or finely chopped
- 3 tsp dried sage or finely chopped fresh
- 1 tsp salt
- ½ tsp ground white pepper
- 150ml (⅔ cup) apple sauce

If you've missed sausage rolls wrapped in buttery, puffy, flaky pastry as much as I have, then you'll have no qualms about making these! Enjoy as a snack, or whip them up whenever you need some party food canapés.

1 Preheat the oven to 180°C fan / 200°C / 400°F.

2 Remove the pastry from the fridge. If the dough feels really firm, leave it at room temperature briefly before rolling. Try not to handle the dough excessively as you work, as this will warm it up and make it more fragile.

3 Add the pork, breadcrumbs, sage, salt and white pepper to a large mixing bowl and mix well, until the mince is as broken down as possible (or use a food processor). Stir in the apple sauce until evenly dispersed. Set aside.

4 Using a floured rolling pin, roll out the pastry on a large sheet of lightly floured non-stick baking parchment into a large rectangle, about 40 x 30cm (16 x 12in) and 3mm (⅛in) thick.

5 With a long side of pastry closest to you, spread the mustard across the centre in a 2.5cm-wide (1in) line, from left to right. Next, spoon the sausagemeat on top of the mustard right up to both side edges. It should be just under 2.5cm (1in) high. Brush one long side of the pastry with beaten egg. Fold the unbrushed side of the pastry over the sausagemeat, then fold the beaten egg side over that. Using your fingers, gently press all along to seal shut, and flip it over so it is seam-side down.

6 Using a sharp knife, cut deep slits into the sausage roll (being careful not to cut all the way through) at 4cm (1½in) intervals. Gently and slowly take both ends of the long sausage roll and bring them together so both ends are touching, creating a circle.

7 Brush the wreath with beaten egg and sprinkle poppy seeds all over the top. Very gently pinch each sausage roll section and lightly twist so it's at an angle, resting on the section behind it.

8 Use the baking parchment to lift the wreath onto a large baking tray, or slide a baking tray underneath it. Bake for 30–35 minutes until golden, then allow to briefly cool on the tray before carefully sliding onto a serving plate. Place a small bowl of cranberry sauce in the middle for dipping.

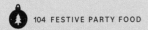

Cheesy Garlic Dough Ball Wreath

 use a thick dairy-free yoghurt, dairy-free cheese and dairy-free Camembert

 use lactose-free Greek yoghurt

 use lactose-free Greek yoghurt and serve no more than 40g (1½oz) Camembert per person

 use extra-mature Cheddar instead of Parmesan

 see the dairy-free advice

Serves 5–6

Takes 40 minutes

- Garlic-infused oil, for greasing and brushing
- 350g (2⅔ cups) gluten-free self-raising (self-rising) flour, plus extra for dusting
- 365g (1¾ cups) Greek yoghurt
- 1 tbsp dried oregano
- 75g (2½oz) extra-mature Cheddar or Parmesan, grated, plus extra to sprinkle
- Pinch of salt
- 1 x 250g (9oz) whole Camembert in a wooden case
- Handful of parsley, finely chopped
- 2 tbsp cranberry sauce

Nothing says Christmas like a wreath of garlic bread dough balls that are crisp on the outside, cheesy, chewy and bready in the middle, dipped in hot cheese with sweet cranberry sauce. This is the festive, tear-and-share crowd-pleaser that us gluten-free folks always miss out on.

1 Preheat the oven to 200°C fan / 220°C / 425°F. Lightly grease a 30cm (12in) ovenproof frying pan or skillet with garlic-infused oil.

2 In a large mixing bowl, combine the flour, yoghurt, oregano, grated cheese and salt. Start by mixing well with a spatula, then when it forms chunky breadcrumbs, get your hands in there to form a big ball of dough. Split the dough in half.

3 Use your hands to roll one half of the dough on a large piece of lightly floured non-stick baking parchment into a long sausage shape, 2.5cm (1in) thick. Using a sharp knife, cut it into 13 or 14 small pieces of dough. Roll each piece in the palms of your hands into a smooth ball. Repeat with the other half of the dough.

4 Place the Camembert in the middle of the pan (lid and packaging removed so only the wooden base remains) and place the dough balls all around the edge. Brush the dough balls with garlic-infused oil and sprinkle with a little extra cheese – as much or as little as you'd like.

5 Bake in the oven for 20 minutes or until the dough balls are golden on top, then cover loosely with foil and cook for a further 5–10 minutes. The timing may vary slightly depending on how big or small you made the dough balls; poke them with a skewer and if it comes out clean, they're done.

6 To finish, brush with a little extra garlic-infused oil and scatter over the parsley. Add small dollops of the cranberry sauce on top before serving warm.

CHEAT'S
Vol-au-vents

D
use dairy-free cream cheese instead of cream cheese and ricotta, and use a smoked dairy-free cheese instead of mozzarella

LL
use lactose-free cream cheese instead of cream cheese and ricotta

F
use lactose-free cream cheese instead of cream cheese and ricotta

VE
follow the dairy-free advice and use 1 tbsp finely chopped chives instead of salmon

Makes 20

Takes 25 minutes

- 1 x 280g (10oz) store-bought gluten-free puff pastry sheet
- Vegetable oil, for greasing

For smoked salmon cream cheese

- 3 tbsp cream cheese
- 1 slice of smoked salmon, finely chopped
- Small handful of dill

For spinach and ricotta

- Small handful of spinach, roughly chopped
- 3 tbsp ricotta
- 1 tbsp finely chopped chives

For tomato and mozzarella

- 5 tbsp passata (sieved tomatoes)
- ½ tsp dried oregano
- Pinch each of salt and ground black pepper
- 3 tbsp finely chopped mozzarella
- 6 small basil leaves

This is one of the first things I made when gluten-free puff pastry popped up in supermarkets for the first time, and I've made them every Christmas since. This recipe guides you as though you were making 6 of each variation. You'll need a mini muffin tray to make these, but a regular one will suffice; your vol-au-vents will just be larger and you'll need to cut out 9cm (3½in) circles of pastry. This will also mean fewer vol-au-vents, but fortunately this recipe is super-easy to double.

1 Remove the pastry sheet from the fridge 10 minutes before starting – this makes it easier to unroll without it breaking or cracking. Preheat the oven to 200°C fan / 220°C / 425°F and lightly grease the holes of a 24-hole mini muffin tray with vegetable oil.

2 Use a 6cm (2¼in) plain round cookie cutter to cut out 20 circles of pastry, then remove the excess. Place each of the circles into the mini muffin tray holes, gently pressing down to loosely line the hole.

3 Bake in the oven for 10 minutes until risen and puffy, then remove and allow to cool for 10 minutes. Either use the end of a wooden spoon to compact down the puffy lid to create small cups, or use a small sharp knife to create a hole that the filling can be spooned into.

4 For the smoked salmon and cream cheese filling, combine the cream cheese and chopped smoked salmon in a small bowl.

5 For the spinach and ricotta filling, place a medium pan over a medium heat. Briefly wash the spinach, add to the pan and cook until wilted, then drain and allow to cool for 10 minutes. Squeeze out any excess water, then combine with the ricotta in a small bowl.

6 For the tomato and mozzarella filling, add the passata, dried oregano, salt and pepper and mozzarella to a small saucepan and place over a medium heat. Simmer for 5 minutes until thickened.

7 Spoon the fillings into the vol-au-vent cases, then top the salmon and cream cheese vol-au-vents with small sprigs of dill, the spinach and ricotta vol-au-vents with chives and the tomato and mozzarella vol-au-vents with small basil leaves.

Cheesy Pesto Christmas Tree

D use dairy-free pesto, cream cheese and grated dairy-free cheese

LL use lactose-free cream cheese and pesto

F use lactose-free cream cheese and low FODMAP pesto

V ensure the pesto is veggie-friendly

VE see dairy-free advice and brush with a sweetened almond milk instead of egg

Serves 7–8

Takes 30 minutes

- 2 x 280g (10oz) store-bought gluten-free puff pastry sheets
- 3 tbsp cream cheese
- 3 tbsp green pesto, plus extra to dollop
- 1 egg, beaten
- 10 sweety drop red peppers (from a jar), drained
- Small handful of grated mozzarella

Here's an easy-peasy, tear-and-share party-food favourite that never fails to impress, filled with oozing creamy cheese and pesto, sandwiched between layers of golden puff pastry. If you've got a lot to prepare, then this recipe is always a great choice as it only requires 10 minutes of actual effort!

1 Remove the pastry sheets from the fridge 10 minutes before starting – this makes it easier to unroll them without breaking or cracking.

2 Preheat the oven to 200°C fan / 220°C / 425°F. Unroll one of the pastry sheets and place on a baking tray lined with non-stick baking parchment, discarding any paper it was rolled in.

3 Mix together the cream cheese and pesto in a small bowl, then spread it over the first pastry sheet. Unroll the second puff pastry sheet and place on top of the first.

4 Using a long, sharp knife (a long ruler helps to keep things straight), cut the layered pastry into the shape of a Christmas tree with a base trunk 5cm (2in) thick. Use a 5cm (2in) star-shaped cutter to cut out 4–5 stars from the excess pastry. Take the remaining pastry offcuts and place to one side for now – you can always bake it after as a chef's treat!

5 Next, with the trunk of the tree closest to you, use a sharp knife to cut 2cm (¾in) branches on both sides of the tree. Cut lines on each side, but stop around 1cm (½in) before the middle.

6 Gently pinch and twist each branch a couple of times, so they look like mini cheese twists – you'll only be able to twist the small branches once. Brush the tree with beaten egg and place the pastry stars on the very top of the tree and down the centre. Brush the stars with egg too.

7 Spoon pesto on top in small dollops to create pesto baubles and adorn with the sweety drop peppers (pointy side upwards). Next, sprinkle over the grated mozzarella.

8 Bake for 20 minutes, or until risen and golden brown, covering loosely with foil once it starts to look golden. Remove from the oven and allow to cool for 5–10 minutes before transferring to a serving board. Add a few more small dollops of pesto, as though they were pesto baubles.

Christmas Lunch

Dad's 'Excell-ent' Turkey

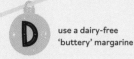 **D** use a dairy-free 'buttery' margarine

 LL

 **F** use garlic-infused oil instead of minced garlic

Serves 10-12

Takes 4 hours

- 1 turkey, 5.5-6.5kg (12-14lb), ideally Norfolk Black or Bronze
- 300g (10½oz) gluten-free pork stuffing (such as my gingerbread stuffing on page 124)
- 2 sprigs of fresh rosemary
- 2 sprigs of fresh thyme
- 2 large dried bay leaves
- 2 clementines, halved
- 1 lemon

For the lemon butter

- 80g (⅓ cup) butter, softened
- 1 tsp minced garlic paste or 2 tbsp garlic-infused oil
- Zest and juice of 1 lemon
- Generous pinch each of salt and ground black pepper

Ever since I can remember, my dad has been in charge of the Christmas turkey, from picking it up, preparing it, basting it, carving and even personally placing the slices on our plates. Though this probably makes him out to be our very own personal chef, he actually rarely cooks a single thing the rest of the year unless it's on the BBQ! However, that doesn't seem to hinder him serving up the world's best, golden turkey that's super-moist and succulent every year without fail. Oh, and in case you didn't realize, it's 'Excell-ent', because that's his surname too!

Before Christmas

1 If your turkey has been frozen, place it in the fridge 4 days before Christmas on the bottom shelf in a suitably sized container. For a larger turkey, allow 10-12 hours of defrosting in the fridge per kilogram/2 pounds, as a general rule.

2 Take the turkey out of the fridge on Christmas eve to ensure it's at room temperature the following day. Cooking a fridge-cold turkey means the outside will be done and start getting dry before the inside is safe to eat, so make sure that doesn't happen!

On Christmas day

3 Remove the stuffing from the fridge about an hour before using to allow it to come up to room temperature.

4 Preheat the oven to 200°C fan / 220°C / 425°F.

5 In a small bowl, combine the ingredients for the lemon butter.

6 Remove the bag of giblets from inside the turkey. Pull the skin at the neck end of the turkey back to reveal the cavity and loosely spoon in the stuffing – don't pack too much in. Pull the neck skin back over and secure with a small cocktail stick. Turn the turkey round so that the body cavity is facing you, then place the rosemary, thyme and bay leaves, the clementine halves and the whole lemon inside.

Continued...

7 Line the base and sides of a large roasting tin (large enough to fit the turkey!) with foil and place the turkey in it breast-side up. Rub all over with the lemon butter. Loosely cover the entire turkey with foil, ensuring it's tented enough to cover the turkey without the foil actually touching it.

8 Roast in the oven for 30-40 minutes, then lower the temperature to 150°C fan / 170°C / 340°F and roast for a further 3-3½ hours, depending on the size of the turkey. Remove the foil covering the turkey and increase the heat to 180°C fan / 200°C / 400°F and cook for a further 30-40 minutes until nicely golden, basting every 10-15 minutes.

9 Use a digital cooking thermometer to probe the breast and thigh of the turkey (as well as the stuffing in the neck cavity) to ensure it's cooked through; 70°C / 160°F is perfect. Alternatively, pierce the thigh with a skewer to check that the juices run clear.

10 Transfer the turkey to a large wooden board or serving plate, cover with lots of foil and allow to rest for 1-2 hours. This resting time can make the difference between all the juices staying in your turkey or watching them all leak out if carved too soon. Reserve the juices in the bottom of the roasting tin, transfer to a jug (pitcher) and use them to make my homemade gluten-free turkey gravy (opposite).

11 Once rested, carve with a freshly sharpened carving knife.

Homemade Turkey Gravy

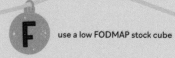

D   LL   F   use a low FODMAP stock cube

Makes 500ml
(generous 2 cups)

Takes 15 minutes

- 400–450ml (generous 1⅔ cups) turkey drippings from the roasting tin
- 4 tbsp cornflour (cornstarch) or gluten-free plain (all-purpose) flour
- 225ml (scant 1 cup) gluten-free chicken stock
- Salt and ground black pepper, to taste

This recipe purely exists because the drippings left behind after roasting a turkey are just too good to waste. Though you'll find a super-simple gravy recipe in my first book which you can make ahead of time, this recipe is just as fast to make once you've harvested those precious turkey juices. Plus the flavour here is very hard to match.

1 Use a tablespoon to skim most of the fat off the top off the reserved juices from the drippings in the jug (pitcher), leaving about 5 tablespoons' worth of fat. Transfer the remaining juices to a small saucepan. Place the saucepan over a low heat, add the flour and mix in until it disappears.

2 Add the stock, stir and simmer for 5–10 minutes until it reduces to a thickened gravy. Season with salt and pepper to taste.

Tip: You can also easily make your own stock from the giblets provided with your turkey instead of using chicken stock. Simply place the giblets, 1 carrot and 1 celery stick (both roughly chopped), 1 small onion or leek (quartered) and 1 bay leaf in a large saucepan. Cover with 1 litre (2 pints) boiling water and simmer for 1–1½ hours, then strain, reserving the stock. Measure out the required amount for this recipe and save the rest for cooking with your festive leftovers.

Freezable: Once cooled, freeze in an airtight container for up to 6 months.

Proper *Bread Sauce*

D
use dairy-free milk, a dairy-free 'buttery' spread and a dairy-free alternative to double cream

LL
use lactose-free milk and lactose-free cream

F
use leek (green parts only) instead of onion, lactose-free milk and lactose-free cream

V

VE
follow the dairy-free advice

Serves 5–6

Takes 20 minutes

- ⅓ leek (100g/3½oz) or 1 small onion, finely chopped
- ¼ tsp black peppercorns
- 50g (3½ tbsp) butter
- 500ml (generous 2 cups) milk
- 2 dried bay leaves
- 3 small slices (115g/4oz) of gluten-free bread
- Pinch of ground cloves
- ¼ tsp ground nutmeg
- Pinch of salt
- 3 tbsp double (heavy) cream

Freezable: Once cooled, freeze in an airtight container for up to 3 months.

Despite being a British classic, bread sauce wasn't a thing in our household at Christmas. But when I went to Uni in Manchester and shared Christmas dinner with my flatmates, I finally got to try it; I couldn't imagine having another Christmas without splodging it on top of my turkey. Sadly, the next year I became gluten-free, then didn't enjoy it again for about five years! Happy ending: I eventually found that even the most questionable gluten-free bread makes the perfect bread sauce and it's now back on my plate for good. Either make ahead and keep chilled or follow the freezing instructions below and once defrosted, rewarm in the microwave.

1 Add the leek/onion, peppercorns, butter, milk and bay leaves to a large saucepan and place over a low-medium heat. Simmer for 15 minutes (don't allow to bubble), stirring occasionally.

2 Blitz the bread in a food processor into fine breadcrumbs. Strain the milk mixture through a sieve into a large jug (pitcher) and discard the solids. Pour the infused milk back into the empty pan (ensure there's no leek/onion left in there) and place back on the heat.

3 Stir in the breadcrumbs and simmer for 2–3 minutes or until you have a thickened, slightly lumpy sauce. Stir in the ground cloves, nutmeg, salt and cream, and serve.

SLOW-COOKER
Peppercorn Beef

 D a dairy-free 'buttery' spread and a dairy-free alternative to double cream

 LL use lactose-free cream

 F use only the green parts of the leek, lactose-free cream and a low FODMAP stock cube

Serves 6-7

Takes 3 hours on high or 6 hours on low

- 2 tsp dried rosemary
- 1 tsp salt
- 2 tsp ground black pepper
- 1 x 1.5–2kg (3½–4½lb) slow-roasting beef joint, such as silverside (top round)
- 1 tbsp butter
- 2 tbsp cornflour (cornstarch)
- 1 leek, chopped into thick chunks
- 100ml (generous ⅓ cup) red wine
- 250ml (generous 1 cup) beef stock
- 2 tbsp brandy
- 1 tbsp black peppercorns
- 3 tbsp double (heavy) cream

Making Christmas lunch so often involves an oven that's full to bursting, so if you're looking for an alternative to turkey that won't take up any valuable oven space, then this is the recipe for you. The beef comes out so tender that it just falls apart, then the peppercorn sauce is hastily made from the liquid it was cooking in.

1 Combine the dried rosemary, salt and 1 teaspoon of the ground black pepper in a small bowl, then rub all over the beef joint.

2 Place the butter, cornflour, leek, wine, stock, brandy, peppercorns and remaining ground black pepper in a slow cooker. Stir well until no lumps of flour are visible, ignoring the fact that the butter is still in a lump.

3 Place the beef joint in the slow cooker. Pop the lid on and cook on low for around 6 hours or on high for 3 hours. Timings may vary a little depending on the size of your slow cooker.

4 Remove the beef and transfer to a serving board. Pass the ingredients left in the slow cooker through a sieve into a small saucepan. Simmer until thickened, then stir in the cream and serve in a jug (pitcher) alongside the beef.

Freezable: Once cooled, freeze in an airtight container for up to 3 months.

Mark's *Sticky Cola Ham*

D

LF

F use leek (green parts only) instead of onion and maple syrup instead of honey

Serves 10

Takes 15 minutes
+ 3 hours cooking time

- 1 smoked or unsmoked boneless gammon joint, 1.8–2.2kg (4–5lb)
- 1.75 litres (3¾ pints) cola (ensure gluten-free)
- 2 large carrots, chopped into 2cm (¾in) chunks
- 1 small leek or onion, roughly chopped
- 1 cinnamon stick
- 2 dried bay leaves
- 4 tbsp gluten-free soy sauce
- 500–750ml (2–3 cups) gluten-free ham stock

For the glaze

- 100ml (generous ⅓ cup) maple syrup or honey
- 50ml (3½ tbsp) black treacle
- 1 tbsp sesame oil
- 1 tsp red miso paste (ensure gluten-free)
- 2 tbsp Chinese five-spice powder
- 3 tbsp rice wine vinegar

Mark and I have always bought a big ol' ham every Christmas, but looking back, all I can really say about it is... it just tasted like nice ham! So here's Mark's new way of spicing things up a bit, using the natural acidity of cola to tenderize the pork, then coating with a sticky, sweet miso and five-spice glaze.

1 Place the gammon in a large flameproof, ovenproof pot that has a lid, then add the cola. Add the carrots, leek/onion, cinnamon stick, bay leaves, soy sauce and as much stock that's required to almost completely cover the gammon joint – this will vary depending on how wide your pot is.

2 Pop the lid on, place over a medium heat and bring to the boil, then reduce the heat down to low and simmer for 2 hours.

3 Preheat the oven to 160°C fan / 180°C / 350°F.

4 Mix all the ingredients for the glaze in a jug (pitcher).

5 Drain and discard the liquid and boiled vegetables and place the gammon in a foil-lined roasting tray. Use a sharp knife to carefully slice off and discard the top layer of skin and a little of the fat, leaving only a thin layer of fat. Score the fat with a sharp knife, creating a criss-cross pattern.

6 Spoon or brush a third of the glaze onto the ham, ensuring generous, even coverage. Place in the oven for 20 minutes, then remove and spoon/brush on another third of the glaze, before returning to the oven for another 20 minutes. Remove and spoon/brush on the remaining glaze and return to the oven for a final 15 minutes.

7 Allow to rest for 10–15 minutes before slicing.

Tip: Some cheaper brands of cola actually aren't gluten-free because they contain barley, so make sure you check the ingredients of yours before using this recipe.

Freezable: Once cooled, slice and freeze in an airtight container for up to 3 months.

Gingerbread Stuffing Log

D use a 'buttery' dairy-free margarine instead of butter

LL

Serves 9–10

Takes 1 hour 20 minutes

- 3 tbsp butter
- ½ medium leek or 1 small onion, finely chopped
- 500g (1lb 2oz) minced (ground) pork
- 1 tsp salt
- ½ tsp ground black pepper
- Grated zest of 1 orange
- 150g (5oz) apple sauce
- 2 slices of gluten-free gingerbread cake (page 68)
- 6 slices of smoked streaky bacon

Freezable: Once cooled, freeze in an airtight container for up to 3 months.

Gluten-free stuffing is (thankfully) one of the few things that is readily available across supermarkets in the UK. However, all I ever wanted for Christmas since I started a gluten-free diet was Nigella Lawson's gingerbread stuffing. It's been well over 10 years since I last ate it, so I finally made my own gluten-free version, inspired by hers. As you'll need to make the gingerbread cake on page 68 first, I've made sure that this part of the recipe is as effortless as possible.

1 Add the butter to a large frying pan and place over a medium heat. Once melted, add the leek or onion and fry until softened, then take off the heat.

2 Place the pork in a large mixing bowl, add the salt and pepper and mix well with a wooden spoon until smooth. Add the orange zest and apple sauce, then mix in well. Add the leek/onion mixture to the bowl and mix in once again.

3 Crumble the gingerbread cake into small chunks into the bowl with your hands (not to the point where it resembles breadcrumbs!). Gently mix in until evenly dispersed.

4 Place a large sheet of cling film (plastic wrap) on a work surface, then lay the strips of bacon side by side on top, very slightly overlapping. Spoon the stuffing mixture on top of the bacon in a long log shape in the middle of the bacon sheet. Compact the stuffing using your hands or a wooden spoon, or there will be no hope that your bacon will fit around it - making a thinner, longer stuffing log will help this too.

5 Lift one side of the cling film and wrap the bacon over the top of the stuffing log, then peel back the cling film and lay it flat again. Repeat on the other side, but don't peel back the cling film this time; instead, tightly wrap the opposite side of cling film back over to seal the log and then tightly seal the ends.

6 Once sealed in cling film, gently roll it on a work surface with your hands to compact the stuffing a little more, and form a neater log shape. Place on a plate in the fridge for 10 minutes to firm up – at this point you can keep it chilled if making it ahead of time.

7 Preheat the oven to 160°C fan / 180°C / 350°F. Line a large baking tray with foil.

8 Place the stuffing log on the prepared baking tray and carefully unwrap, making sure not to lift it too much or it can easily break. Ensure the log is placed so the seam of bacon is underneath it, then cover the tray tightly with foil.

9 Bake in the oven for 30 minutes, then remove the foil and return to the oven for a final 20 minutes. Allow to rest for 10 minutes before transferring to a serving plate, slicing and serving.

To make gingerbread stuffing balls

- If making stuffing balls, you won't need the bacon. After mixing the gingerbread cake into the stuffing mixture, use an ice-cream scoop to take heaped portions of it and compact it into the scoop with your palm. Turn out onto the prepared baking tray and repeat until you've used up all of the mixture.

- Take each portion into your hands and gently roll to form a perfect ball, then space apart evenly on the tray. Bake in the oven at 160°C fan / 180°C / 350°F for 25 minutes until golden brown. Alternatively, place in an air fryer set at 200°C / 400°F for 10 minutes until golden brown.

To stuff a turkey

- Omit the bacon, and once the gingerbread cake has been mixed into the stuffing mixture, use it to stuff your turkey following the instructions on page 114. Roll any leftovers into stuffing balls and follow the timings above to bake.

BRIE AND CRANBERRY *Nut Roast*

D use a dairy-free 'buttery' margarine and omit the Brie

LL

V

VE follow the dairy-free advice and use 2 flax eggs (see page 27) instead of the eggs

Serves 6–8

Takes 1 hour

- 75g (2½oz) dried cranberries
- 50g (1¾oz/2–3 small slices) gluten-free bread
- 150g (5oz) mixture of shelled pistachios and pecans
- 2 tbsp dried sage or 5–6 fresh sage leaves, finely chopped
- 2 tbsp butter
- 1 medium leek, finely chopped
- 200g (7oz) mushrooms, finely chopped
- 1 tbsp smoked paprika
- 125g (4½oz) dried red lentils (ensure gluten-free)
- 375ml (generous 1½ cups) gluten-free vegetable stock
- 100g (3½oz) Brie, chopped into chunks, plus an extra 40g (1½oz), sliced, to serve
- 2 large eggs
- Salt and ground black pepper
- 2 tbsp cranberry sauce, to serve

For the roasted vegetables
- 2 tbsp garlic-infused oil
- 350g (12oz) peeled butternut squash, cut into 2cm (¾in) cubes
- 1 red (bell) pepper, deseeded and cut into 3cm (1¼in) chunks

If your opinion of nut roasts is that they're dry and tasteless, then this recipe is here to change your mind. Not only is it wonderfully crisp on the outside yet crunchy and moist (like a nutty, roasted vegetable stuffing) in the middle, but the flavour is indisputable. This is a nut roast for veggies and meat eaters alike!

1 Preheat the oven to 180°C fan / 200°C / 400°F. Line a 900g (2lb) loaf tin (pan) with non-stick baking parchment.

2 Add the cranberries, bread, pistachios and pecans, and sage to the mixer. Blitz briefly until everything is broken up, but stop before blitzing into a fine dust! Set aside for later. Alternatively, prepare by hand by simply using a large sharp knife to chop everything up as finely as possible. Set aside.

3 Generously grease a large baking tray with the garlic-infused oil.

4 Add the squash and red pepper to the tray and mix around until everything is well coated. Roast in the oven for 25–30 minutes or until slightly blackened at the edges. Season with a pinch each of salt and pepper.

5 Melt the butter in a large saucepan over a medium heat, then add the leek and mushrooms, frying for 5 minutes or until the mushrooms start to soften. Add the smoked paprika and fry for 2–3 more minutes. Add the lentils and stock and bring to the boil. Simmer for 10 minutes or until all of the liquid has been absorbed and the lentils have swelled. Remove from the heat.

6 Add the blitzed/chopped cranberry mixture to the pan, followed by the chopped Brie. Stir well until everything is evenly dispersed, then crack in both eggs and stir until combined. Season with a pinch each of salt and pepper.

7 Lastly, stir in the roasted vegetables, transfer the mixture to the prepared loaf tin and compact down well with a silicone spatula. Tightly cover with foil and roast in the oven for 35 minutes, then remove the foil and roast for another 20 minutes or until the top is golden brown.

8 Allow to rest for 10 minutes before turning out onto a serving plate and removing the baking parchment. Serve topped with cranberry sauce and slices of Brie.

Freezable: Once cooled, freeze in an airtight container (don't top with cheese and cranberry sauce until serving) for up to 1 month.

ULTIMATE MUSHROOM  Wellington

 D LF V VE

brush with almond milk instead of egg

Serves 6

Takes 1 hour

- 1 tbsp garlic-infused oil
- 500g (1lb 2oz) mushrooms, sliced
- 100g (3½oz) leek, finely chopped
- 150g (5oz) cooked and peeled chestnuts, chopped
- 115g (4oz) spinach, finely chopped
- 2 tbsp cranberry sauce
- 2 tbsp miso paste (ensure gluten-free), or 3 tbsp gluten-free soy sauce
- 4 fresh sage leaves, finely chopped
- Salt and ground black pepper
- 2 x 280g (10oz) packs store-bought gluten-free puff pastry
- 1 egg, beaten, to glaze

Freezable: Once cooled, freeze in an airtight container for up to 3 months.

Meet the ultimate mushroom wellington: starring light, crisp and golden puff pastry and a hearty mushroom filling tinged with sage, cranberry sauce, leek and chunky chestnuts. It's fit for any Christmas dinner plate, whether you're a meat eater or not.

1 Place a large pan over a medium heat and add the garlic-infused oil. Add the mushrooms and leek and fry until softened and the moisture released from the mushrooms has cooked off. Stir through the chopped chestnuts and spinach and fry until the spinach wilts. Add the cranberry sauce, miso paste or soy sauce, sage leaves and salt and pepper to taste. Mix well to combine, then remove from the heat and allow to cool completely.

2 Preheat the oven to 180°C fan / 200°C / 400°F. Line a baking tray with non-stick baking parchment. Remove the pastry from the fridge 10 minutes before assembly – this makes it easier to unroll.

3 Lay one sheet of puff pastry on the baking parchment and pile the mushroom mixture on top in the middle of the pastry in a rectangular shape, leaving a border around the edge. Ensure that it's fairly compact but has good height.

4 Brush a little water around the pastry border, then place the other sheet of puff pastry on top. Use your hands to gently but tightly shape it around the filling, then trim any excess pastry so that you have a 2cm (1in) pastry border around the edge. Keep the trimmed pastry to one side, as we will use this later! Crimp the border of your wellington with a fork to secure the filling.

5 Use a sharp knife to cut 3 slashes across the top of the wellington, then brush all over with beaten egg. Use a star-shaped cutter to cut stars out of the excess pastry and stick them on top. Brush these with egg too. Bake in the oven for about 45 minutes until golden all over. If it is darkening too quickly, lightly cover with foil for the remainder of the cooking time.

To cook in the air fryer

- Preheat the air fryer to 200°C / 400°F. Place the wellington in the air fryer for 14-16 minutes until the pastry is golden and crisp.

6 Remove from the oven or air fryer, allow to rest for about 5 minutes, then slice and serve with gluten-free vegetable gravy and veggies.

BROCCOLI AND CAULIFLOWER CHEESE *Tart*

 D

use a 'buttery' dairy-free margarine, dairy-free milk and a smoked dairy-free cheese that melts well

 LL

use lactose-free cream and milk

V

Serves 6

Takes 1 hour + cooling

- 1 quantity of ultimate gluten-free shortcrust pastry (page 204) or use store-bought
- 150g (5oz) cauliflower florets (about ½ large cauliflower), cut into bite-sized chunks
- 100g (3½oz) broccoli florets (about ½ small broccoli head), cut into bite-sized chunks
- 75g (2½oz) leek, chopped into chunks
- 40g (1½oz) extra-mature Cheddar, grated
- 2 tbsp gluten-free breadcrumbs
- Salt and ground black pepper

For the cheese sauce

- 2 tbsp butter
- 2 tbsp gluten-free plain (all-purpose) flour
- 250ml (generous 1 cup) milk
- 60g (2oz) extra-mature Cheddar, grated
- 1 tsp wholegrain mustard (optional)
- 2 medium eggs

Freezable: Once cooled, freeze in an airtight container for up to 3 months.

My mum's famous broccoli and cauliflower cheese is such a crowd-pleasing side at Christmas that I decided to transform it into a creamy, cheesy veggie main event, encased in golden, flaky pastry. So if you're not a nut roast kind of person, then there's a high likelihood that this will be right up your street!

1 Remove the pastry from the fridge; if it feels really firm, leave it out at room temperature briefly before rolling it. Remember not to handle the dough excessively as you work with it, as this will warm it up and make it more fragile. Lightly flour your rolling pin. On a large sheet of non-stick baking parchment, roll out the dough to a 2mm (⅛in) thickness, into a large circular shape.

2 Transfer the pastry to a 23cm (9in) fluted tart tin (pan). I do this by supporting the pastry as I gently invert it into the tin, with equal overhang on all sides. Peel off the baking parchment. Next, use your fingers to carefully ease the pastry into place, so that it neatly lines the tin. Lift the overhanging pastry and, using your thumb, squash 2mm (⅛in) of pastry back into the tin. This will result in slightly thicker sides which will prevent the pastry case from shrinking when baked.

3 Allow the overhang to do its thing – we'll trim the overhang after chilling it. Lightly prick the base of the pastry case with a fork, then place in the fridge for 15 minutes.

4 Preheat the oven to 180°C fan / 200°C / 400°F. Place a large baking tray in the oven.

5 Use a rolling pin to roll over the top of the tart tin, instantly removing the overhang and flattening down the pastry. Next, loosely line the base of the pastry case with baking parchment and fill with baking beans (or uncooked rice if you don't have any). Place on the preheated baking tray in the oven and cook for 15 minutes.

Continued...

6 Remove the baking parchment and baking beans and bake for a further 5 minutes. Remove from the oven and allow to fully cool.

7 Place the cauliflower in a large saucepan, fill the pan just under halfway with boiling water, then bring to the boil over a medium heat. Once boiling, cook for 5 minutes, then add the broccoli and leek and cook for a further 3 minutes. Drain and set aside.

8 While the veg is cooking, prepare the cheese sauce. Add the butter, flour and milk to a large saucepan and mix in thoroughly so that the flour is no longer visible and lumpy. Place over a medium heat until the butter has melted, then turn the heat down to low. At this point, you need to keep stirring it until it has transformed into a lovely, thick sauce, about 5-10 minutes.

9 Stir in the grated cheese and mustard, if using, then season with salt and pepper to taste. Allow to cool for 10 minutes before cracking in the eggs and quickly stirring in to create a thinner, glossy sauce.

10 Spoon the drained cauliflower, broccoli and leek into the pastry case and pour the sauce all over. Top with the grated cheese and breadcrumbs and cook in the oven (on the baking tray) for 25 minutes or until the top is nicely browned and crisp.

11 Allow to cool for 5 minutes before removing from the tin and serving warm, with a dollop of cranberry sauce on top.

Sticky Maple Orange Parsnips & Carrots

D · LF · F · V · VE

Serves 4-5

Takes 1 hour

- 4 tbsp vegetable oil
- 3 medium carrots, trimmed and peeled
- 3 medium parsnips, trimmed and peeled
- 5 tbsp maple syrup
- 1½ tbsp wholegrain mustard
- Grated zest of 1 orange and 2 tbsp juice

If you want to level up both your carrots and parsnips this Christmas (and get them both done at the same time) then this recipe will be right up your street. Every bite is crisp, with a sticky, sweet maple orange glaze and a tang of mustard. (Pictured on page 137.)

1 Preheat the oven to 180°C fan / 200°C / 400°F. Add the vegetable oil to a large baking tray, tilt the tray to spread it out evenly, then place in the oven.

2 Cut the carrots and parsnips into strips around 1-1.5cm (½-⅔in) thick and 5cm (2in) long, ensuring they are all about equal in size so they cook evenly and at the same speed.

3 Spread out the carrots and parsnips on the preheated tray in a single layer, mix around until coated in the oil and roast for 35 minutes until lightly browned.

4 Meanwhile, make the glaze by mixing the maple syrup, mustard, orange zest and juice in a jug (pitcher).

5 Remove the tray from the oven and drizzle the glaze over the veg, then turn everything until well coated. Place back in the oven for a further 10-15 minutes or until any sauce left on the tray has become thick and sticky (leave it too long and it'll burn and stick to the tray). Remove from the oven and give everything one last stir so that there's no sticky sauce left on the tray.

To cook in the air fryer

- Preheat the air fryer to 200°C / 425°F, then pop in the carrots and parsnips to fry for about 15 minutes, turning over 2-3 times during the cooking time. For the final 5-7 minutes, drizzle with the glaze and mix until everything is well coated.

Tip: This recipe also works really well with honey in place of the maple syrup.

Freezable: Once cooled, freeze in an airtight container for up to 6 months.

SUPER-CRISPY

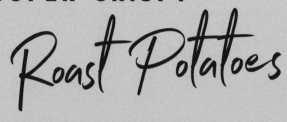

Roast Potatoes

D   LF   F   V

use vegetable oil

VE

use vegetable oil

Serves 4–6

Takes 40 minutes

- 1kg (2lb 3oz) Maris Piper potatoes, peeled and chopped into 4cm (1½in) chunks
- Vegetable oil or goose fat
- Small handful of fresh rosemary or thyme (optional)
- Salt

Freezable: Once parboiled and shaken, allow to fully cool then freeze for up to 6 months. Once defrosted, continue from step 5.

When everything disappeared from my Christmas lunch plate on starting a gluten-free diet, these golden roast potatoes were always there for me. Each roast potato is super-crispy thanks to the 'fluffing up' technique, something that I'm pretty sure I'll be doing for the rest of my life now – they just turn out so crunchy on the outside and fluffy in the middle!

1 Preheat the oven to 200°C fan / 220°C / 425°F.

2 Bring a large saucepan of boiling salted water to the boil, then add the potatoes. Boil for about 10 minutes, starting from the point at which the water is bubbling, until the pieces are softer on the outside but still firm in the middle.

3 Once the potatoes are boiling, place a large roasting tray in the oven with a generous amount of oil or goose fat in it.

4 Drain the potatoes and transfer back into the pan, then pop the lid on. Shake the pan a good few times to fluff up the outside (you can't be too violent!), which helps to attain a crispy exterior once roasted.

5 Place the potatoes on the hot tray in the oil or fat, making sure they're in a single layer; they should sizzle. Either quickly turn all of the potatoes over on the baking tray so the oil or fat is covering all sides, or drizzle a little extra oil on top.

6 Roast in the oven for 40 minutes, then turn the potatoes over, sprinkle with fresh rosemary or thyme, if using, and pop them in the oven for a further 10–15 minutes until crisp and golden.

7 Season with a little salt and serve.

To cook in the air fryer

- Preheat the air fryer to 200°C / 425°F, then add the parboiled potatoes and air fry for 20 minutes, turning over 2–3 times during the cooking time.

3-INGREDIENT
Bacon Brussels Sprouts

D **LF** **F** **V** **VE**

F: serve no more than 50g (1¾oz) Brussels sprouts per person

V: swap the bacon for 100g (3½oz) chestnuts (finely diced, cooked and peeled), adding them along with the pine nuts

VE: see vegetarian advice

Serves 5-6

Takes 40 minutes

- 3 tbsp vegetable oil
- 1kg (2lb 3oz) Brussels sprouts, trimmed
- 5 slices of smoked streaky bacon, finely diced
- 60g (2oz) pine nuts

As a kid, the mere sight of a Brussels sprout filled me with terror, but this is the dish that made me realize how much I'd been missing out on them. The crispy, smoky bacon and distinctively nutty pine nuts complement the roasted sprouts so well that even sprout dodgers like me will be asking for these every year. After all, when you're gluten-free, you don't get the luxury of turning down foods that are naturally gluten-free!

1 Preheat the oven to 200°C fan / 220°C / 425°F. Drizzle the oil over a large baking tray.

2 Bring a large saucepan of water to the boil and add the sprouts. Cook for 4-5 minutes, then drain, cover with cold water and drain once more.

3 Add the sprouts and bacon to the prepared tray. Toss the sprouts and bacon in the oil so they're well coated and nicely mixed up.

4 Roast in the oven for around 15 minutes, then turn all the sprouts over and scatter on the pine nuts. Continue to roast for 5-10 minutes until the sprouts are a little golden, the pine nuts are nicely toasted and the bacon is crispy.

To cook in the air fryer

- Preheat the air fryer to 200°C / 425°F, then add the sprouts and bacon for about 10 minutes. Turn everything over, then add the pine nuts and air fry for a further 5 minutes.

Freezable: Once cooled, freeze in an airtight container for up to 6 months.

Mum's Red Cabbage

 D LF F V VE

use only the green parts of the leek instead of shallots; one serving is a safe low FODMAP serving size

Serves 12

Takes 10 minutes
+ 2½ hours cooking time

- 1 large red cabbage (900g/2lb)
- 400g (14oz) shallots or 1 large leek, finely chopped/blitzed in a food processor using the grating/shredding attachment
- 1 very large cooking apple (400g/14oz), such as Bramley, peeled, cored and finely chopped/blitzed in the food processor using the grating/shredding attachment
- 2 tbsp garlic-infused oil
- Grated zest of 1 orange
- ¼ tsp Chinese five-spice powder
- ¼ tsp ground nutmeg
- ¼ tsp ground cloves
- 1 tsp salt
- ¼ tsp ground white pepper
- 3 tbsp dark brown sugar
- 3 tbsp red wine vinegar

I can't imagine Christmas without my mum's sweet, sour, subtly spiced red cabbage on the side of my plate. This recipe is the ultimate definition of 'tried and tested' when you consider that my mum has made this annually for 30 years!

1 Preheat the oven to 140°C fan / 160°C / 325°F.

2 Remove the outer leaves of the cabbage and cut into quarters. Remove the hard white stem and centre and blitz in a food processor using the disc slicer attachment. Alternatively, use a sharp knife or mandoline to slice into shreds.

3 Transfer the cabbage to a large Dutch oven or ovenproof casserole dish with a lid. Mix through the shallots or leek and the apple. Add the remaining ingredients and stir well until everything is well coated. Pop the lid on and bake in the oven for 2½ hours, stirring 2–3 times during cooking.

To cook in the slow cooker

- Place the prepared ingredients in a slow cooker, stir well until everything is well coated and pop the lid on. Cook on high for 4–5 hours or on low for 6–7 hours until tender, stirring 2–3 times during cooking. Timings may vary a little depending on the size of your slow cooker.

Freezable: Once cooled, freeze in an airtight container for up to 6 months.

Ultimate Potato Gratin Dauphinoise

 D use a 'buttery' dairy-free margarine, dairy-free milk and a smoked dairy-free cheese that melts well

 LL use lactose-free milk

 F use lactose-free milk and only the green parts of the leek instead of onion

V

 VE see dairy-free advice

Serves 8

Takes 20 minutes + 1 hour 20 minutes cooking time

- Butter, for greasing
- 1kg (2lb 3oz) potatoes, peeled and sliced into discs 3mm (⅛in) thick
- 1 small onion or ½ large leek, finely chopped

For the white sauce

- 2 tbsp butter
- 2 tbsp garlic-infused oil
- 3 tbsp gluten-free plain (all-purpose) flour or cornflour (cornstarch)
- ½ tsp ground nutmeg
- 750ml (generous 3 cups) milk
- 150g (5oz) extra-mature Cheddar, grated
- Salt and ground black pepper

Freezable: Once cooled, slice into portions and freeze in an airtight container for up to 1 month.

Meet the side that's so good, you'll want to fill half of your plate with it. After all, with layers of perfectly roasted scalloped potatoes in a thick, creamy, cheesy sauce, it's hard to limit such a wondrous creation to the sidelines, isn't it? There's no need to pre-cook the potatoes for this – they cook straight from raw – making it surprisingly quick to prepare. I've never met a person who hasn't loved this dish!

1 Preheat the oven to 180°C fan / 200°C / 400°F. Lightly grease a 33 x 28cm (13 x 11in) ovenproof dish with butter.

2 For the sauce, add the butter, garlic-infused oil, flour, nutmeg and milk to a large saucepan and mix thoroughly so that the flour is no longer visible and lumpy. Place over a medium heat until the butter has melted, then turn the heat down to low. At this point, you need to constantly stir until it has transformed into a slightly thickened sauce, about 5–8 minutes.

3 Add the grated cheese and mix in, then season with a pinch each of salt and pepper. Remove from the heat and set aside.

4 Create a layer of potatoes in the bottom of the oven dish, so that they slightly overlap at the edges. Generously season with a big pinch each of salt and pepper, then scatter over half the onion or leek.

5 Pour half the sauce on top and spread into an even layer, then create the final layer using the remaining potato slices, again slightly overlapping at the edges. Season generously with salt and pepper and scatter over the remaining onion/leek. Pour on the remaining sauce and spread to create an even layer.

6 Cover loosely with foil (if the foil touches the top, it will get stuck!) and bake in the oven for 1 hour. Remove the foil and bake for a further 20 minutes.

Tip: You can also make this in a smaller 28 x 18cm (11 x 7in) dish without any alterations to the quantities. Simply create three layers of potato slices topped with leek/onion and salt and pepper in the dish, with a third of the sauce in between each layer and on top. Bake for the same time, but keep an eye on it during the final 20 minutes as it may brown faster.

3-INGREDIENT
Yorkshire Puddings

 D use dairy-free milk

 LF use lactose-free milk

 F use lactose-free milk

 V

Makes 12

Takes 30 minutes

- Vegetable oil
- 200g (1⅔ cups) cornflour (cornstarch)
- 6 eggs
- 300ml (1¼ cups) milk

Though not technically a traditional staple of Christmas lunch, if these aren't on my plate then something has gone very wrong! Even Nigella Lawson approved of these, which means you now have absolutely no excuse for these not to grace your plate.

1 Preheat the oven to 200°C fan / 220°C / 425°F.

2 Grab a 16-hole muffin tray and add just under 1 tablespoon of oil to each of the holes. Place in the preheated oven for 10–15 minutes until the oil is super-hot – basically spitting!

3 Meanwhile, grab a large mixing bowl and add the cornflour. Crack in the eggs and whisk together.

4 Once thoroughly combined, gradually add all of the milk, a little at a time, whisking in between. Pour the batter into a jug (pitcher) so it's easier to pour into each hole.

5 Next, you need to be quick! Remove the muffin tray from the oven and immediately fill each hole with the mixture until just under three-quarters full. They should sizzle a little as you pour the batter in. Get them back in the oven ASAP!

6 Bake for 15–20 minutes until golden and risen; do not open the oven door or they will instantly deflate! Once you can see that they're huge and fully risen, give them an extra 2 minutes to crisp up, as this will reduce the amount they deflate once you remove them from the oven.

7 Serve up immediately.

Tip: You can also use tapioca starch instead of cornflour. Don't overfill your holes with too much oil or too much mixture. Both of these things will impact the ability for the Yorkshires to rise and crisp up. Less is more!

Freezable: Once cooled, freeze in an airtight container for up to 3 months.

Desserts

Brandy Snap Baskets

D use a hard dairy-free alternative to butter

LL

V

VE see dairy-free advice

Makes 12

Takes 40 minutes

- 55g (¼ cup) light brown sugar
- 55g (2 tbsp) golden syrup
- 55g (3½ tbsp) butter
- 50g (6 tbsp) gluten-free plain (all-purpose) flour
- ½ tsp ground ginger (optional)
- ½ tsp lemon juice
- Ice cream, chocolate sauce and fresh berries (optional), to serve

Tip: These are perfect for making ahead. Once cooled, store in an airtight container for up to 5 days, ready for spontaneous serving.

This was my favourite dessert as a kid, and I have many happy memories enjoying it after a pub lunch with my Ouma. They used to serve it filled with vanilla ice cream, fresh berries and chocolate sauce, though for some reason I used to pick the berries out. I now realize the error of my ways and add extra berries to make up for it. Fill them however you like, but I'd highly recommend filling with my Christmas leftovers ice cream (page 200) for the ultimate experience.

1 Preheat the oven to 160°C fan / 180°C / 350°F. Line a large baking tray with non-stick baking parchment.

2 Measure the sugar, syrup and butter into a small saucepan and place over a low heat, stirring constantly and ensuring it doesn't boil, until the butter has melted and the sugar has fully dissolved, about 10 minutes.

3 Remove from the heat and allow to sit for a minute before adding the flour and ground ginger, if using. Mix quickly so that it combines well and the flour doesn't clump. Immediately add the lemon juice and give it a good mix.

4 Use a teaspoon to spoon 3–4 round dollops of the mixture onto the prepared baking tray (1 teaspoon per dollop). Make sure they are quite far apart from each other as they will spread out a lot. Bake in the oven for about 12 minutes until they're golden, spread and have an almost lacy look to them.

5 Remove from the oven and allow to rest for a couple of minutes before using a palette knife to ease off one of the brandy snaps – work quickly from this point, but don't rush! Once you've carefully removed your super-flexible brandy snap from the parchment, flop it over the top of an upside-down drinking glass. Have a few glasses ready so you can do multiple at a time.

6 Once firmed up, remove the brandy snap baskets from the glasses and place on a wire rack. If any firm up too much before you get the chance to shape them, pop them back into the oven for a few seconds and they will soften again enough to shape.

7 Continue using up the mixture to make more – it can firm up very quickly in the pan, so pop it over a low heat again to loosen it, and once at the consistency it was before, repeat with the round dollops. Use a new piece of baking parchment if you need to.

8 Serve each basket with any or all of the following: a dollop of Christmas aftermath ice cream (page 200) and a drizzle of chocolate sauce and some fresh berries, if you like.

White Chocolate and Gingerbread Cheesecake

D

use a hard dairy-free margarine, white chocolate, cream cheese (minimum 23% fat), and double (heavy) cream (minimum 30% fat)

LL

use lactose-free white chocolate, cream cheese and lactose-free whipping cream (minimum 30% fat)

F

see low-lactose advice

V

VE

see dairy-free advice

Serves 8–10

Takes 30 minutes + 5 hours chilling

For the base
- 320g (11¼oz) gluten-free ginger biscuits (cookies)
- 150g (⅔ cup) butter, melted

For the filling
- 500g (2¼ cups) mascarpone
- 100g (¾ cup) icing (confectioners') sugar
- 1 tbsp ground ginger
- 300ml (1¼ cups) double (heavy) cream
- 250g (9oz) white chocolate, melted and just cooled

To decorate
- 100ml (⅓ cup plus 1 tbsp) double (heavy) cream
- 1 tbsp icing (confectioners') sugar
- 50g (1¾oz) white chocolate, grated
- 8 mini gluten-free gingerbread men
- 50g (1¾oz) gluten-free ginger biscuits (cookies), crushed

The combination of sweet white chocolate, creamy cheesecake filling and warming, slightly fiery gingerbread is something I look forward to every year. Best of all, it's no-bake, so it's super-easy to prepare ahead of time and chill until you're ready to serve.

1 First make the base. In a food processor, blitz the biscuits to a crumb-like texture – not into a fine dust! Alternatively, pop the biscuits into a zip-lock bag and bash them with a rolling pin. Add to a large bowl and pour in the melted butter. Mix well.

2 Spoon the mixture into a round 20cm (8in) loose-bottomed or springform cake tin (pan). Compact it into the base in an even layer, then chill in the fridge while you make the filling.

3 I use a stand mixer to make the filling, but you can easily do this using an electric hand whisk. Doing it by hand is achievable, but in that case, it's vital that you whisk long enough (as you're far more likely to undermix by hand).

4 Place the mascarpone, icing sugar and ground ginger into the bowl of the stand mixer. Mix on a low–medium speed for 10–20 seconds, then add the cream. On a medium speed, mix for 2 more minutes or until it begins to firm up. Pour in the melted white chocolate and briefly mix until combined. Do not overmix, as the mixture can split; it should end up as a nice, thick, spoonable consistency, not a pourable one.

5 Spread the filling evenly on top of the chilled biscuit base and place into the fridge to chill for at least 5 hours, but ideally overnight.

6 When ready to serve, whip the cream and icing sugar together in a large mixing bowl until stiff – an electric mixer is best here. Transfer to a piping (pastry) bag with an open star nozzle.

7 Carefully remove the cheesecake from the tin and transfer to a serving plate. Pipe 8 blobs of whipped cream all around the edge of the cheesecake. Sprinkle over the grated white chocolate and top each blob of cream with a mini gingerbread man. Sprinkle the remaining crushed ginger biscuits in the middle of the cheesecake.

Freezable: Once chilled and set (but before piping on fresh cream), slice or leave whole, then freeze in an airtight container for up to 3 months.

Not-a-Christmas-pudding

 D use a dairy-free margarine, chocolate and double cream (minimum 30% fat)

 LL use lactose-free chocolate and cream (minimum 30% fat)

 F see low-lactose advice

V

Serves 6–8

Takes 30 minutes
+ 2½ hours steaming time

For the pudding

- 120g (1 cup minus 1½ tbsp) gluten-free self-raising (self-rising) flour
- 1 tsp gluten-free baking powder
- ¼ tsp xanthan gum
- 30g (4 tbsp) unsweetened cocoa powder
- 150g (¾ cup) caster (superfine) sugar
- 1 tsp vanilla extract
- 150g (⅔ cup) butter, softened
- 3 medium eggs

For the chocolate sauce

- 150g (5oz) chocolate, broken into pieces
- 150g (5oz) double (heavy) cream
- 1 tsp vanilla extract
- 25g (1oz) golden syrup

It has to be said that I'm not the biggest fan of traditional Christmas pudding... and I know I'm not alone here! However, what I would opt for is this ridiculously tasty steamed chocolate pudding. It almost looks like a Christmas pudding... but it ain't! The chocolate sauce is divine and pairs well with any other desserts over Christmas too.

1 Grease a 1-litre (2-pint) pudding basin and place a circle of non-stick baking parchment in the base.

2 Add all the ingredients for the pudding to a large mixing bowl and mix until well combined. Tip into the prepared pudding basin and pop a lid on it. If your pudding basin doesn't have a lid, create one by cutting a circle of foil and baking parchment roughly 4cm (1½in) larger than the basin's diameter. Place both circles on top of one another and create a pleat down the middle. Secure this lid to the basin using string and use extra string to create a handle, if you can – this will make lifting it out of the pan later easier.

3 Place in a large saucepan and add boiling water so that it comes a third of the way up the pudding basin. Place the lid on the pan, bring to the boil and simmer gently over a low heat for 2–2¼ hours. Keep an eye on the water level as you may need to add some more if it's getting low.

4 For the sauce, place all the ingredients in a pan and gently heat, stirring and making sure it doesn't boil, so everything is melted. Once melted, remove from the heat and mix until well combined – the sauce should be a perfect consistency and ready to use straight away. It can also be reheated if made ahead of time and any excess sauce can be kept in the fridge and reheated when needed.

5 When ready to serve, turn the pudding onto a plate, remove the circle of baking parchment and pour over the hot chocolate sauce.

Freezable: Once cooled, freeze the sauce and the pudding in separate airtight containers for up to 3 months.

Black Forest Yule Log Trifle

 D make the chocolate icing dairy-free, use dairy-free custard, chocolate and cream (minimum 30% fat)

 LL make the chocolate icing low lactose, use lactose-free custard, chocolate and cream (minimum 30% fat)

V

Serves 8–10

Takes 1 hour

For the sponge layer

- 1 gluten-free chocolate yule log (page 54; omit the orange extract)
- ½ quantity of chocolate icing (page 54; omit the orange extract) or 300ml (1¼ cups) double (heavy) cream whipped with 2 tbsp icing (confectioners') sugar
- 50ml (3½ tbsp) Kirsch

For the custard layer

- 500ml (generous 2 cups) shop-bought custard (ensure gluten-free)
- 100g (3½oz) dark chocolate, broken into small pieces

For the whipped cream layer

- 600ml (2½ cups) double (heavy) cream
- 2 tbsp icing (confectioners') sugar
- 2–3 tbsp Kirsch

For the cherry filling layer

- 1 x 400g (14oz) can of cherry pie filling
- 2 tbsp Kirsch

To finish

- 30g (1oz) dark chocolate, grated
- 8 fresh cherries

What would Christmas day be without a trifle? Sadly, most gluten-free people would probably be able to answer that question! This chocolate yule log and boozy cherry trifle suits a medium-sized trifle dish, but I know everyone's are different, so you may need a little more or a little less of any of the components, depending on the size of yours.

1 First, make the yule log sponge (page 54) leaving out the orange extract. Once cooled while rolled up, unroll and spread with the chocolate icing and re-roll OR use the whipped cream. Leave the outside uncovered.

2 For the chocolate custard layer, place the custard and chocolate in a saucepan over a low heat. Heat gently and stir until the chocolate has melted and it's well combined. Remove from the heat and transfer to a bowl, cover with cling film (plastic wrap) and allow to fully cool.

3 For the whipped cream layer, pour the cream into a large mixing bowl and whisk until it reaches soft peaks. Add the icing sugar and mix until well combined, then add the Kirsch and gently fold in.

4 For the cherry filling layer, mix together the black cherry pie filling with the Kirsch.

5 To assemble, slice the yule log into round slices and place slices all around the sides of a trifle dish, as well as in the base as a flat layer. Pour over the Kirsch and allow it to soak into the sponge.

6 Spread a layer of the cherry filling on top of the log layer, then cover with a layer of chocolate custard. Follow this with a layer of the whipped cream, then repeat the layers. Finish with the grated chocolate and cherries as a garnish. Allow to set and chill in the fridge until ready to serve.

Tip: Fancy making this a chocolate trifle? Remove the Kirsch and cherry elements and you're sorted! Feel free to just remove the Kirsch to make it alcohol free too.

Berry and Prosecco Roulade

 D use dairy-free cream (minimum 30% fat)

 LF use lactose-free cream (minimum 30% fat)

 F see lactose-free advice and use any type of berry apart from blackberries

 V use veggie-friendly prosecco

Serves 8

Takes 50 minutes
+ soaking time

- 150g (5oz) berries (raspberries, strawberries, blueberries, blackberries), defrosted if frozen
- 120ml (½ cup) prosecco, plus an extra 2 tbsp for the cream

For the meringue

- 4 large egg whites
- 225g (2 cups plus 2 tbsp) caster (superfine) sugar
- 1 tsp white wine vinegar
- 1 tsp cornflour (cornstarch)
- 50g (½ cup) ground almonds
- 45g (1½oz) flaked (slivered) almonds

For the filling

- 300ml (1¼ cups) double (heavy) cream
- 50g (6 tbsp) icing (confectioners') sugar, plus extra to finish
- 3 tbsp prosecco

Freezable: Once decorated, slice and freeze in an airtight container for up to 3 months.

A roulade for dessert on Christmas day has always been a tradition in our family throughout my teenage years. I hope my mum doesn't mind me saying it, but she never actually made it; we always bought one from the farm shop when we went to collect the turkey! Not only is my re-creation a boozy berry version, but I can also actually eat this one – a roulade isn't always gluten-free, so do always be careful if buying a shop-bought one like we used to.

1 Place the berries in a small bowl and add the prosecco, then leave to soak for 2–3 hours or overnight – the longer you leave them, the stronger the prosecco flavour will be.

2 Preheat the oven to 170°C fan / 190°C / 375°F. Line a Swiss roll tin (pan), 33 x 23cm (13 x 9in), with non-stick baking parchment.

3 In a large mixing bowl, whisk the egg whites to fairly stiff peaks, then gradually add the sugar while still whisking – I prefer to use an electric hand mixer for this. It should become thick and glossy. Next, fold through the vinegar, cornflour and ground almonds, using a silicone spatula, before carefully spooning it into the prepared tin. Spread into an even layer, then sprinkle the flaked almonds evenly over the top.

4 Bake for 25–30 minutes until golden, risen and fairly firm to the touch. Remove from the oven and invert the meringue onto another sheet of non-stick baking parchment. Leave to cool for about 10 minutes.

5 Meanwhile, make the filling. In a large mixing bowl, whip the cream with the icing sugar and gradually add the prosecco – again, I use an electric hand mixer for this. Whip until thick but try not to over-whip.

6 Drain the berries (be sure to enjoy the prosecco they were soaking in!) and chop any larger ones, then fold two-thirds of the berries through the whipped cream, using a silicone spatula.

7 Spread a layer of the whipped cream onto the meringue and then roll the meringue up carefully from a short side, using the baking parchment beneath to help you. It will crack as you go; this is normal and exactly what you want to happen!

8 Decorate with a dusting of icing sugar and the remaining berries.

Tip: You can make this without the prosecco; just omit from the cream and berries to create a berry roulade.

Neapolitan *Baked Alaska*

D

use a hard dairy-free margarine and dairy-free vanilla/chocolate/strawberry ice cream

LL

use lactose-free vanilla/chocolate/strawberry ice cream

F

see low-lactose advice

V

Serves 8

Takes 1 hour + chilling time

- 1 x 2-litre (4¼-pint) tub of Neapolitan ice cream

For the sponge base

- 110g (½ cup minus 1 tsp) butter, softened
- 110g (½ cup plus 1 tbsp) caster (superfine) sugar
- 2 eggs
- ½ tsp vanilla extract
- 85g (⅔ cup minus 2 tsp) gluten-free self-raising (self-rising) flour
- ¼ tsp xanthan gum
- 25g (¼ cup) unsweetened cocoa powder (or swap the same weight for extra flour if you prefer a vanilla sponge)

For the Italian meringue

- 100g (3½oz) egg whites (about 3–4 whites)
- 200g (1 cup) caster (superfine) sugar
- 45ml (3 tbsp) water
- ¼ tsp cream of tartar

I always thought that making a dessert like this would be next to impossible, not because of the gluten-free aspect, but mostly because I imagined it ending in a big pool of melted ice cream! However, it's actually insanely easy to make, and the end result is a dream, with layers of strawberry, vanilla and chocolate ice cream, surrounded by a fluffy, marshmallow-like meringue with a crisp, lightly scorched exterior. I'd highly advise getting a digital food thermometer when making the meringue, otherwise it's very hard to know when the sugar syrup is ready.

1 Remove the ice cream from the freezer so it softens a little. Prepare a small glass mixing bowl (use a bowl somewhere between 18–20cm/7–8in in diameter) by placing 2–3 layers of cling film (plastic wrap) into the bowl with some overhang so the ice cream can be lifted out easily later.

2 Scoop the vanilla ice cream into the base of the bowl and compact it down to create a flat layer – it should be soft enough that you can smooth it over to level it. Pop this (and the ice-cream tub) into the freezer briefly to firm up. Remove the ice cream tub from the freezer again so it softens a little, then layer the strawberry ice cream on top of the vanilla in a flat, compacted layer. Finally, do the same with the chocolate ice cream. Place in the freezer to completely firm up for at least a couple of hours.

3 For the sponge, preheat the oven to 160°C fan / 180°C / 350°F. Grease a 20cm (8in) round cake tin (pan) and line with non-stick baking parchment.

4 In a large mixing bowl, cream together the butter and sugar until light and fluffy – I prefer to use an electric hand whisk for this. Add the eggs, vanilla extract, flour, xanthan gum and cocoa powder, if using. Mix together until combined.

Continued...

5 Spoon the mixture into the prepared tin and bake for 25–30 minutes until risen and cooked through. Remove from the oven and leave the sponge in its tin for about 5 minutes before turning it out onto a wire rack to cool completely. If the sponge isn't a similar diameter to the bowl that the ice cream is currently in, you can trim it down to be the same size, using a sharp knife (though this part is optional as the discrepancy in size can be masked when coated with meringue).

6 I use a stand mixer to make the Italian meringue, but an electric hand whisk will do the job just fine too. If making by hand, ensure you mix for longer, until everything is well-combined and consistent. Place the egg whites in the bowl of a stand mixer with a whisk attachment in place, ready for later.

7 Add the sugar and water to a medium pan and mix until combined and gloopy; try to avoid getting any sugar up the sides of the pan. Place over a medium heat and work quickly from this point onwards. Add the cream of tartar to the egg whites in the stand mixer bowl and whisk on a medium speed until soft peaks form.

8 Once the sugar mixture reaches 118°C (244°F) – I use a digital food thermometer to check – remove from the heat and carefully drizzle the sugar syrup into the stand mixer bowl while the mixer is still running. Try not to get the sugar syrup on the sides of the bowl as it will instantly harden and crystallize. Once all the syrup is combined, continue to whisk until the meringue is stiff, glossy and cooled.

9 Just before serving, place the sponge base on a serving plate (or a large baking tray lined with non-stick baking parchment if you don't have a kitchen blowtorch). Remove the prepared ice cream from the freezer, turn out onto the centre of the sponge and peel off the cling film. Spoon on the Italian meringue until all the ice cream and sponge is covered, creating an igloo shape.

10 Ideally, use a kitchen blowtorch to brown the meringue. If you don't have one, simply pop the baked Alaska into a preheated oven at 220°C fan / 240°C / 465°F for a few minutes until lightly browned. As this contains ice cream, it must be served immediately, as the ice cream will completely melt when left out at room temperature. If you have space in your freezer, it can be stored in the freezer until ready to serve.

Tips: Instead of creating three layers of ice cream, you could simplify things and just use one flavour, which would remove the need to keep refreezing the layers in the bowl.

To clean the saucepan you made your sugar syrup in, simply fill with boiling water. Add in any utensils used too. Bring it to a simmer for 5–10 minutes and all the sugar will magically dissolve into the water. If you use cold water to clean your pan, the sugar syrup will harden and be near impossible to remove!

Freezable: Once blow-torched or baked, freeze in an airtight container for up to 3 months. If you can't find an airtight container the right size, simply slice and freeze in individual freezer bags.

Salted Caramel Pear Frangipane Tart

 D use a hard dairy-free alternative to butter, and dairy-free caramel to drizzle

 LL use lactose-free caramel to drizzle

 V

Serves 8–10

Takes 1 hour 20 minutes

- 1 quantity of ultimate gluten-free shortcrust pastry (page 204)
- 1 egg, beaten
- Small handful of flaked (slivered) almonds
- Generous drizzle of salted caramel sauce (store-bought)

For the frangipane filling
- 2–4 pears
- 125g (scant ⅔ cup) caster (superfine) sugar
- 125g (½ cup plus 1 tbsp) butter, softened
- 2 eggs, beaten
- 125g (1 cup plus 3 tbsp) ground almonds
- 1 tsp almond extract
- 50g (6 tbsp) gluten-free plain (all-purpose) flour
- ½ tsp gluten-free baking powder

I actually don't think I've ever shared a recipe that contains pears before – how crazy is that? Answer: not that crazy, but regardless it just felt right to announce that this is my debut pear pud! The pears go so well with the frangipane, staying super-juicy, and then the sweetness of the salted caramel sauce just brings everything together.

1 Remove the pastry from the fridge; if it feels really firm, leave it out at room temperature briefly before rolling it. Remember not to handle the dough excessively as you work with it, as this will warm it up and make it more fragile. Lightly flour a rolling pin. On a large sheet of non-stick baking parchment, roll out to a 2mm (⅛in) thickness, in a large circular shape.

2 Transfer the pastry to a 23cm (9in) fluted tart tin (pan). I do this by supporting the pastry as I gently invert it into the tin, with equal overhang on all sides. Peel off the baking parchment. Next, use your fingers to carefully ease the pastry into place, so that it neatly lines the tin. Lift the overhanging pastry and, using your thumb, squash 2mm (⅛in) of pastry back into the tin. This will result in slightly thicker sides, which will prevent the pastry case from shrinking when baked. Allow the overhang to do its thing – we'll trim the overhang after chilling it. Lightly prick the base of the pastry case with a fork, then place in the fridge for 15 minutes.

3 Preheat the oven to 180°C fan / 200°C / 400°F.

4 Use a rolling pin to roll over the top of the tin, instantly removing the pastry overhang and flattening down the pastry. Next, loosely line the base of the pastry case with baking parchment and fill with baking beans (or uncooked rice if you don't have any).

5 Bake in the oven for 15 minutes, then remove the baking parchment and baking beans and bake for a further 5 minutes. Remove from the oven, brush the base with beaten egg and pop back in the oven for a couple of minutes. (The egg helps to seal the pastry when filled to prevent it from becoming soggy.) Remove from the oven and allow to cool completely.

Continued...

6 Reduce the oven temperature to 160°C fan / 180°C / 350°F.

7 Peel, core and halve the pears. Hasselback each pear half by slicing three-quarters of the way through all along the pear to create slits, making sure the pear half stays intact.

8 In a large mixing bowl, cream together the sugar and butter until light and pale – I prefer to do this using an electric hand whisk. Add the beaten egg gradually and mix again until combined. Fold in the ground almonds, almond extract, flour and baking powder.

9 Spoon the frangipane mixture into the tart case and spread it out so it's nice and level. Place the prepared pears on top of the frangipane, evenly spaced. You can either have 4 halves (2 pears' worth) or 8 halves (4 pears' worth).

10 Bake in the oven for 45–50 minutes, sprinkling over the flaked almonds about 10 minutes before the tart is done.

11 It is cooked when the frangipane no longer wobbles when shaken. Allow to cool for 5 minutes before serving warm, drizzled with salted caramel sauce.

Tip: This tart would also work well with cooking apples instead of pears too, if you'd prefer.

Freezable: Once cooled, slice or leave whole and freeze in an airtight container for up to 3 months.

Irish Cream No-Bake Tart

Serves 8

Takes 20 minutes
+ 3 hours chilling

For the base
- 350g (12oz) gluten-free digestive biscuits (graham crackers)
- 2 tbsp unsweetened cocoa powder
- 165g (¾ cup) butter, melted

For the filling
- 150g (5oz) milk chocolate
- 150g (5oz) dark chocolate
- 40g (3 tbsp) butter
- 270ml (1 cup plus 2 tbsp) double (heavy) cream
- 130ml (½ cup plus 2 tsp) Irish cream (I use Baileys)

To finish
- 50g (1¾oz) white chocolate, melted
- 25g (1oz) milk chocolate, grated
- 8 gluten-free Irish cream truffles (see page 82 for homemade, or use shop-bought – I use Baileys Chocolate Truffles)

I love making no-bake desserts over Christmas – the oven usually has enough going on, so to make something that doesn't require any of the oven's precious time is glorious. Additionally, no-bake tarts can be made ahead of time, which is a big future time-saver. With a chocolate biscuit base and a luxuriously indulgent Irish cream liqueur filling, this one is an absolute family favourite and never lasts long in our house.

1 In a food processor, blitz the biscuits into a crumb-like texture – not into a fine dust! If you don't have a food processor, pop the biscuits into a zip-lock bag and bash them with a rolling pin. Add the cocoa powder to the biscuits and blitz or mix in once more until the biscuits are a dark chocolate colour. Add to a large mixing bowl and pour in the melted butter. Mix until well combined.

2 Spoon the mixture into a 23cm (9in) loose-bottomed fluted tart tin (pan). Compact the mixture into the base and up the sides of the tin using the back of a spoon. Next, press the base of a small jar or measuring cup over the base and sides to tightly compact, ensuring the sides are a consistent thickness. It should look similar to a chocolate pastry case. Chill in the fridge for at least 30 minutes.

3 To prepare the filling, slice the milk and dark chocolate finely with a sharp knife – this helps it melt more quickly when you pour the cream onto it. Place in a heatproof bowl with the butter.

4 In a small saucepan, heat the cream and Baileys – do this gently until the cream is just about to reach boiling point (I stir mine a little so it doesn't stick to the bottom as it heats up), then pour the mixture on top of the chopped chocolate and butter. Leave for about 5 minutes without stirring, then mix it all together so that it is combined, smooth and fully melted.

5 Remove the tart tin from the fridge. Pour in the filling mixture and spread evenly with a spatula or palette knife. Chill in the fridge for a few hours, or even overnight, to allow the filling to fully set.

6 Finish with a drizzle of melted white chocolate and top with a little grated milk chocolate and truffles.

Freezable: Once decorated, slice or leave whole and freeze in an airtight container for up to 3 months.

Sticky Toffee Apple Pudding

D
use a hard dairy-free butter alternative and dairy-free milk and cream

LL
use lactose-free milk and cream

V

Serves 6–8

Takes 1 hour

- 600g (1lb 5oz) cooking apples, such as Bramley, peeled, cored and chopped
- 1 tbsp lemon juice
- 40g (3¼ tbsp) brown sugar
- 15g (1 tbsp) butter, plus extra for greasing

For the sponge

- 200ml (¾ cup plus 1 tbsp) milk
- 1½ tbsp lemon juice
- 75g (⅓ cup) butter, softened
- 2 medium eggs
- 125g (⅔ cup minus 2 tsp) light brown sugar
- 165g (1¼ cups) gluten-free self-raising (self-rising) flour
- 2 tbsp black treacle
- ½ tsp bicarbonate of soda (baking soda)
- ¼ tsp gluten-free baking powder
- ½ tsp ground ginger
- ½ tsp ground cinnamon

For the sticky toffee sauce

- 115g (generous ¾ cup) light brown sugar
- 1 tbsp black treacle
- 275ml (1 cup plus 2½ tbsp) double (heavy) cream
- 90g (⅓ cup plus 1 tbsp) butter

Year after year, one of the most popular recipes that I see people making for Christmas Day dessert is (insert drum roll here) my sticky toffee pudding. It's a recipe that lives in my very first cookbook and I still love it unconditionally. I wanted to put a spin on that recipe so it could make a return in this book, but in the process of doing so, I think I might have made something even better! Think layers of gooey apple, soft and fluffy spiced sponge, and the same sticky toffee sauce we all know and love.

1 Preheat the oven to 160°C fan / 180°C / 350°F. Grease a rectangular baking tin, 30 x 23cm (12 x 9in), with a little butter.

2 Place the apple, lemon juice, brown sugar and butter in a pan and place over a low–medium heat. Allow the butter to melt and then mix everything so the apple is nicely coated. Heat for 5–10 minutes until the apple is a little softened. Place to one side.

3 In a jug (pitcher), mix the milk with the lemon juice and allow to rest for 10 minutes until it curdles a little.

4 Add all the remaining ingredients for the sponge to a large mixing bowl and whisk together until well combined – I prefer to use an electric hand whisk for this. Slowly add the milk/lemon mixture in 2 stages, whisking in between until well combined.

5 Place the apples in the base of the baking tin and pour the sponge mixture on top. Bake for 35–40 minutes until golden.

6 While it's baking, add all the ingredients for the sticky toffee sauce to a small pan and place over a low heat. Allow the sugar to dissolve and everything to melt down, stirring occasionally. Bring to the boil and stir for 2–3 minutes before removing from the heat. Allow to cool until the sauce reaches a lovely, pourable and sticky consistency.

7 Remove the pudding from the oven, portion it up and then serve with the sticky toffee sauce. You can also additionally (or alternatively to the sauce) serve with gluten-free custard.

Freezable: Once cooled, freeze the sauce and the pudding in separate airtight containers for up to 3 months.

LEMON CURD
Baked Cheesecake

V

Serves 12

Takes 30 minutes + cooling + 12 hours chilling

For the base

- 320g (11¼oz) gluten-free digestive biscuits (graham crackers)
- 150g (⅔ cup) butter, melted

For the filling

- 600g (2⅔ cups) full-fat cream cheese
- 30g (3⅔ tbsp) gluten-free plain (all-purpose) flour
- 185g (1 cup minus 1½ tbsp) caster (superfine) sugar
- 3 eggs, beaten
- Grated zest of 3 lemons and juice of 1
- 175g (6oz) sour cream

For the lemon curd (or use store-bought)

- 2 large eggs
- Grated zest and juice of 2 lemons
- 115g (½ cup) butter
- 160g (¾ cup plus 1 tbsp) caster (superfine) sugar

Freezable: Once cooled and topped with lemon curd, slice or leave whole, then freeze in an airtight container for up to 3 months.

There's something about the creamy texture of a baked cheesecake that can't be beaten, and when you combine that with my lemon curd... it's cheesecake heaven. You can use store-bought curd if you want, but my homemade version is better (and really easy to make too).

1 To make the base in a food processor, blitz the biscuits to a crumb-like texture - not into a fine dust! If you don't have a food processor, pop the biscuits into a zip-lock bag and bash them with a rolling pin. Add to a large mixing bowl and pour in the melted butter. Mix until well combined. Spoon the mixture into a round 20cm (8in) loose-bottomed or springform cake tin (pan). Compact it into the base in an even layer. Chill the base in the fridge for at least 30 minutes while you make the filling.

2 Preheat the oven to 200°C fan / 220°C / 425°F.

3 I use a stand mixer for the filling, but an electric hand whisk will work too. If making by hand, ensure you mix for longer, until everything is well combined. Place the cream cheese in a stand mixer and mix on a low speed for 1 minute. In a small bowl, mix the flour and sugar, then gradually add it to your mixer, maintaining the low speed. Next, gradually add the beaten eggs along with the lemon zest and juice. Turn the mixer off and fold in the sour cream by hand. Evenly spread the filling on top of the chilled biscuit base.

4 Bake for 10 minutes, then drop the temperature to 90°C fan / 110°C / 200°F and cook for a further 30–35 minutes. Once cooked, it should be wobbly and a little brown around the edges. Instead of removing it from the oven, leave it in, turn the oven off and keep the door shut for 30 minutes.

5 After 30 minutes, open the door of the oven ajar to allow the cheesecake to cool slowly. This will prevent cracking in the top of the cheesecake. Leave to cool for 2–3 hours. Once cooled, cover the tin in foil (around the edges and underneath too), then place in the fridge to chill for 12 hours.

6 For the lemon curd, crack the eggs into a medium saucepan and beat. Add the lemon zest and juice, butter and sugar, then place over a medium heat. Whisk the mixture, allowing the butter to melt, then cook, whisking, for 8–10 minutes without letting it boil, until the curd starts to thicken slightly. Allow to cool completely before popping it into a glass jar to thicken further in the fridge.

7 To serve, remove the cheesecake from the tin and spread a layer of lemon curd on top.

Profiterole Wreath

D use dairy-free milk, chocolate and cream (minimum 30% fat)

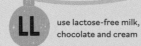

LL use lactose-free milk, chocolate and cream

F see lactose-free advice

V

Makes 36-40 choux buns

Takes 45 minutes
+ cooling time

- 1 quantity of gluten-free choux pastry (page 204)
- Handful of gluten-free festive sprinkles
- 50g (1¾oz) white chocolate, grated

For the crème pâtissière filling

- 180g (6½oz) egg yolks (about 10-12 yolks)
- 60g (½ cup) cornflour (cornstarch)
- 150g (¾ cup) caster (superfine) sugar
- 750ml (3 cups) whole milk
- 1 tbsp vanilla extract

For the chocolate ganache

- 175g (6oz) dark or milk chocolate, finely chopped
- 175ml (¾ cup) double (heavy) cream

Though I enjoy profiteroles all year round, they're still just as essential at Christmas to me as my go-to Christmas playlist. After all, when I was younger, a shop-bought mound of them would suddenly appear in the fridge as a 'just in case we need another dessert' insurance policy! So here's my festive tribute to profiteroles, made with homemade choux pastry and filled with crème pâtissière, neatly arranged into an awe-inspiring wreath.

1 For the filling, in a large mixing bowl, beat the egg yolks to break them all up, then add the cornflour and half the sugar. Mix thoroughly to combine, then set aside.

2 Add the milk, vanilla extract and remaining sugar to a medium saucepan and whisk until well combined. Place the pan over a low heat until it just starts to boil, then immediately pour a third of the mixture into the egg mixing bowl and whisk constantly to combine. Follow this with another third of the milk, whisking once more until well incorporated.

3 Pour the contents of the mixing bowl back into the saucepan (with the remaining third of the milk) and whisk constantly over a medium heat until it thickens. It will be frothy on top to start with, but as it starts to thicken, this will disappear and a lovely thick custard will develop – turn the heat to low at this point. Keep whisking constantly until you see large bubbles form on top of the custard. This lets you know that the cornflour is cooked and the custard is ready.

4 Remove from the heat and transfer the custard to a bowl to cool. Cover with cling film (plastic wrap) so that it is touching the surface of the custard; this will prevent a skin from forming as it cools. Place in the fridge for 2-3 hours to cool completely and thicken further.

5 Preheat the oven to 190°C fan / 210°C / 410°F. Line two baking trays with non-stick baking parchment.

6 If you haven't already, transfer the gluten-free choux pastry dough into a piping (pastry) bag fitted with a 1cm (½in) round nozzle. If you don't have a piping bag, you can simply spoon it onto the baking trays instead.

7 Pipe balls that are 5cm (2in) in diameter onto the prepared baking trays, leaving a 2cm (¾in) space between each ball. Wet your finger and dab the top of each ball to help round them off, gently smoothing over any pointy bits.

8 Bake in the oven for 25-30 minutes; don't open the oven door during this time. Remove from the oven, flip the buns over, pierce the bottom of each with a skewer to let the steam out and pop back in the oven for a further 5 minutes, upside down. Turn the oven off and leave in the oven with the door ajar to cool down gradually.

9 You have two choices of how to fill the profiteroles. Either slice them in half and spoon (or pipe) the filling in as though you were assembling a sandwich, or place your crème pâtissière in a piping bag fitted with a long filler nozzle and pipe it in from the bottom of the bun until it starts to feel heavier and full.

10 For the ganache, put the chocolate into a large mixing bowl. Heat the cream in a small saucepan until just before it begins to boil, then pour over the chocolate and leave to stand for 5 minutes before mixing together until smooth. Briefly cool and then dip the top of the filled choux buns into the ganache.

11 Arrange the profiteroles in a wreath shape on a serving plate while the ganache is still wet. Place a few profiteroles on top of the wreath base to create a second layer, then sprinkle over the festive sprinkles and grated white chocolate.

Tips: Don't have time make the crème pât? Simply whip up 600ml (2½ cups) double (heavy) cream and use instead.

Fancy making a smaller profiterole wreath? Simply halve the recipe to create a wreath that serves 4.

Freezable: Ideally freeze once the profiterole shells have cooled but before you have filled them; bake them briefly once defrosted to restore their crisp exterior, then continue with the recipe as normal. If this isn't possible, feel free to freeze them once they are filled and the ganache is set. Freeze in an airtight container for up to 3 months.

Mini Christmas Puddings

D use a hard dairy-free alternative to butter

LL

V

Makes 3 x 500ml (1 pint) puddings

Takes 45 minutes
+ soaking time
+ 5½ hours steaming time

- 150g (5oz) raisins
- 150g (5oz) currants
- 150g (5oz) candied mixed peel
- 1 small cooking apple, such as Bramley, peeled, cored and roughly chopped
- Zest and juice of 1 lemon
- 4 tbsp brandy or sherry, plus an extra 4 tbsp to serve
- 75g (⅓ cup) butter, softened
- 150g (¾ cup) light muscovado sugar
- 2 large eggs
- 90g (⅔ cup) gluten-free plain (all-purpose) flour
- 1 tsp gluten-free baking powder
- ½ tsp xanthan gum
- 1 tsp ground nutmeg
- 2 slices of gluten-free bread, blitzed into breadcrumbs

For the brandy butter

- 125g (generous ½ cup) butter, softened
- 200g (scant 1½ cups) icing (confectioners') sugar, sifted
- 4 tbsp brandy
- Grated zest of ½ orange

Two of the most common questions I get asked about my Christmas pudding recipe (in my second book) are: how do I make multiple smaller Christmas puddings in a 1-pint tin? And how long do I steam them for? In case you didn't know, the original recipe was for one big Christmas pudding, so here I give timings and instructions to make 3 smaller puddings instead.

1 Place the raisins, currants, mixed peel and apple in a large bowl. Add the lemon zest and juice and brandy or sherry. Allow to stand for a minimum of 2 hours, or ideally overnight. The longer the better!

2 Grease three 500ml (1 pint) pudding basins and line the bases with circles of non-stick baking parchment. If your pudding basins don't have a lid, create them by cutting three circles of foil and baking parchment that are roughly 3cm (1¼in) larger than the basin's diameter. Place one foil circle and one paper circle on top of one another and create a pleat down the middle. Repeat twice more and set aside.

3 In a large mixing bowl, cream together the butter and sugar, then add the eggs one at a time, mixing between additions. Add the flour, baking powder, xanthan gum, nutmeg and breadcrumbs and mix until well combined. Lastly, stir through all of the soaked fruit, along with the soaking liquid, and mix once more.

4 Divide the mixture between the prepared pudding basins, ensuring that the mixture is flat and even on top by compacting it down. Secure the lids in place. If you made the lids from foil and baking parchment, use some string to secure them in place. If your pudding basins came with lids, I'd recommend wrapping each in foil after popping it on, just to be safe.

5 Place all three puddings in a large saucepan and add boiling water so that it comes just over a third of the way up the basins. Place the lid on the pan, bring to the boil and simmer for 4 hours. Keep an eye on the water level, as you may need to top it up halfway through.

Continued...

6 Once cooked, remove the pudding basins from the water, remove the lids and allow to cool completely in the basins. Once cool, cover and store in a cool, dry place until Christmas day.

7 On Christmas day, pop the lids on your pudding basins – if you made your own, you'll need to create them again. Place in a large saucepan again and fill once again with boiling water, just over a third of the way up the pudding basins. Pop the lids on, bring to the boil and simmer for 1½ hours.

8 While they are steaming, whip up the brandy butter. I use a stand mixer for this, but an electric hand whisk will do the job just fine too. If making by hand, just ensure you mix for longer. Place the butter in the bowl of a stand mixer and mix on a medium speed for about 5 minutes until a lot paler. Add the icing sugar and mix until completely incorporated, then add the brandy and orange zest and mix once more. Transfer the puddings to individual serving plates and keep the brandy butter refrigerated until you serve everything up.

9 To serve, warm up the extra 4 tablespoons of brandy in a small saucepan (don't let it boil) and then pour a little over the hot Christmas puddings. Carefully set light to each and serve immediately with the brandy butter.

Freezable: Once steamed and cooled, freeze in an airtight container for up to 1 year. Once defrosted, continue with the second steam.

Mince Pie Mug Cake

 **D** use dairy-free milk

 **LF** use lactose-free milk

 V

Makes 1 mug cake

Takes 5 minutes

- 2 tbsp caster (superfine) sugar
- 4 tbsp gluten-free plain (all-purpose) flour
- ½ tsp ground mixed spice
- 2 tbsp vegetable oil
- 1 egg yolk
- 2 tbsp milk
- ½ tsp gluten-free baking powder
- 2 tsp mincemeat (see page 46 for homemade)
- 1 tsp icing (confectioners') sugar, for dusting
- Gluten-free custard or ice cream, to serve

Over the festive period I find there are so many cosy evenings where I'm sitting at home, wrapping presents or watching a Christmas movie and I fancy a little pud... but equally can't be bothered to make anything! And here's my go-to solution. The sponge is super-fluffy, lightly spiced with two healthy dollops of mincemeat – perfect with a scoop of ice cream or a splash of custard.

1 Put all the ingredients except the mincemeat, icing sugar and custard or ice cream into a microwaveable mug (mine holds about 300ml/1¼ cups). Mix together until combined with a fork.

2 Add the mincemeat to the top and push it down a little so it goes beneath the cake mixture.

3 Cover tightly with cling film (plastic wrap) and pierce a hole in the top, then pop into the microwave on high (mine is 900W) for 60–70 seconds.

4 Remove from the microwave, dust with the icing sugar and serve with custard or ice cream.

Tip: Feel free to swap the mincemeat for raspberry or strawberry jam to cater for any mince pie dodgers.

Millionaire's No-Bake Cheesecake Pots

D
use dairy-free cream cheese (minimum 23% fat), dairy-free cream (minimum 30% fat) and dairy-free chocolate and caramel

LL
use lactose-free cream cheese, lactose-free cream (minimum 30% fat) and lactose-free chocolate and caramel

F
see lactose-free advice

V

see dairy-free advice

VE
see dairy-free advice

Makes 6

Takes 30 minutes
+ 1–2 hours chilling

For the base
- 150g (5oz) gluten-free shortbread or digestive biscuits (graham crackers)
- 50g (3½ tbsp) butter, melted

For the filling
- 350g (1½ cups) full-fat cream cheese or mascarpone
- 50g (6 tbsp) icing (confectioners') sugar
- ½ tsp vanilla extract
- 50g (1¾oz) canned caramel, plus extra to finish
- 150ml (⅔ cup) double (heavy) cream

For the ganache top
- 100g (3½oz) dark or milk chocolate, finely chopped, plus an extra 25g (1oz), grated, to finish
- 100g (3½oz) double (heavy) cream

Freezable: Once chilled, freeze in freezer-friendly ramekins in an airtight container for up to 3 months.

Individual desserts are just what we need sometimes, agreed? And what's great about these is that they can be made ahead of time and just sit in the fridge ready and waiting to be served. Making no-bake cheesecakes in little pots like this massively reduces the chilling time needed, as it doesn't have to hold itself up, so it can be perfect for a fairly last-minute dessert too.

1 In a food processor, blitz the biscuits to a crumb-like texture – not into a fine dust! Alternatively, pop the biscuits into a zip-lock bag and bash them with a rolling pin. Add to a large mixing bowl, pour in the melted butter and mix well.

2 Divide the base mixture evenly between 6 ramekins, spooning it in and then pressing it down firmly to form a base. Place in the fridge to chill while you make the filling.

3 Place the cream cheese or mascarpone, icing sugar and vanilla extract in a (cleaned) large mixing bowl – I prefer to use an electric hand mixer for this. Mix on a low-medium speed for 10–20 seconds, add the canned caramel and mix in briefly before adding the cream. Mix until it begins to firm up; it shouldn't take more than a minute or so. Definitely don't overmix, as the mixture can split.

4 Divide the cheesecake mixture evenly between the ramekins. Fill it up a little lower than the top of the ramekin, leaving a little space for the ganache topping. Pop in the fridge to chill and firm up for 1–2 hours.

5 To make the ganache, place the chocolate in a bowl. Gently heat the cream in a saucepan until just before it boils, then pour the hot cream over the chocolate and leave for about 5 minutes. Stir the chocolate and cream together until combined and smooth.

6 Pour over the top of the cheesecakes, pushing it out to the sides so it's nice and level. Place back in the fridge for another 45–60 minutes.

7 Once ready to serve, remove from the fridge, drizzle with a little extra caramel and sprinkle over the extra grated chocolate.

Ouma's Pecan Pie

D   LL   V

Serves 12

Takes 1 hour 20 minutes
+ 2 hours setting

- 1 quantity of ultimate gluten-free shortcrust pastry (page 204)
- 65g (¼ cup plus 1 tsp) butter
- 190g (1 cup minus 1 tbsp) light brown sugar
- 190ml (½ cup plus ½ tbsp) golden syrup
- 3 large eggs, plus 1 extra beaten egg for brushing
- 1 tsp cornflour (cornstarch)
- 1 tsp vanilla extract
- ½ tsp salt
- 200g (7oz) pecans, chopped
- Gluten-free custard, to serve

Freezable: Once cooled, slice or leave whole and freeze in an airtight container for up to 3 months.

I'm so grateful I got to share so many moments with my Ouma (my South African grandma) when I was growing up... and when I think about it, so many of those moments involved a slice of pecan pie! So this recipe is my tribute to her, as it never fails to take me back to all those times that still make me smile many years later. Oh, and make sure you allow this to cool for a few hours before slicing - it makes all the difference!

1 Remove the pastry from the fridge; if it feels really firm, leave it out at room temperature briefly before rolling it. Remember not to handle the dough excessively as you work with it, as this will warm it up and make it more fragile. Lightly flour a rolling pin. On a large sheet of non-stick baking parchment, roll out the pastry to a 2mm (⅛in) thickness, into a large circular shape.

2 Transfer the pastry to a 23cm (9in) fluted tart tin (pan). I do this by supporting the pastry as I gently invert it into the tin, with equal overhang on all sides. Peel off the baking parchment.

3 Next, use your fingers to carefully ease the pastry into place, so that it neatly lines the tin. Lift the overhanging pastry and, using your thumb, squash 2mm (⅛in) of pastry back into the tin. This will result in slightly thicker sides, which will prevent the pastry case from shrinking when baked. Allow the overhang to do its thing - we'll trim the overhang after chilling. Lightly prick the base of the pastry case with a fork, then place in the fridge for 15 minutes.

4 Preheat the oven to 180°C fan / 200°C / 400°F.

Continued...

5 Once chilled, use a rolling pin to roll over the top of the tin, instantly removing the overhang and flattening down the pastry. Next, loosely line the base of the pastry case with baking parchment and fill with baking beans (or uncooked rice if you don't have any). Bake in the oven for 15 minutes, then remove the parchment and baking beans and bake for a further 5 minutes. Remove from the oven, brush the base with beaten egg and pop back in the oven for a couple of minutes. The egg helps to seal the pastry when filled to prevent it from becoming soggy. Allow to cool completely and reduce the temperature to 160°C fan / 180°C / 350°F.

6 For the filling, melt the butter, sugar and syrup in a small saucepan over a low heat. Allow to simmer for a minute or so, then remove from the heat and leave to cool for 10 minutes.

7 Whisk the eggs briefly in a bowl with the cornflour, vanilla extract and salt. Gradually add the cooled butter and sugar mixture, whisking as you add it to ensure the eggs have no chance to cook (the mixture should be cool enough by now anyway!). Stir in the chopped pecans and pour the mixture into the prepared pastry case.

8 Bake for 50 minutes or until puffed up and less wobbly. Remove from the oven and allow to cool for a couple of hours until set. Slice and serve with custard, just how Ouma used to like it!

Festive Leftovers

MARK'S LEFTOVER
Turkey Curry

D — use dairy-free 'buttery' margarine

LL

F — use parsnips and carrots, leek instead of onion (green parts only), use low FODMAP stock and omit the mango chutney

V — use a 400g (14oz) can of chickpeas (drained) instead of the leftover turkey and use vegetable stock

VE — combine the dairy-free and vegetarian advice

Serves 4

Takes 20 minutes

- 1 tbsp garlic-infused oil
- 2 tbsp butter
- 1 small onion or 50g (1¾oz) leek, finely chopped
- 250–350g (9–12oz) leftover cooked turkey, chopped into bite-sized chunks
- 200–250g (7–9oz) leftover cooked veg (such as parsnips, carrots, broccoli or sprouts)
- 700ml (scant 3 cups) gluten-free ham or chicken stock
- 2 tbsp mango chutney
- Small handful of coriander (cilantro)

For the spice blend

- 1 tbsp curry powder
- ½ tsp ground cinnamon
- ½ tsp ground ginger
- ¼ tsp dried chilli flakes
- 1½ tbsp cornflour (cornstarch)

This curry couldn't be quicker or easier to make, and if you love it as much as I do, you can happily make it all year round to use up leftover chicken and veggies whenever you like. It's mildly spicy, with a unique flavour depending on which veg you throw in, and a sweet finish thanks to the mango chutney.

1 In a small bowl combine all the ingredients for the spice blend. Set aside.

2 Place a large pan over a medium heat and add the garlic-infused oil and butter. Once the butter has melted, add the onion or leek and fry for 3 minutes.

3 Add the leftover turkey and veg, followed by the spice blend. Fry until fragrant, then add the stock. Simmer for 10 minutes or until nicely thickened, then add the mango chutney and stir in.

4 Finish by topping with fresh coriander leaves, and serve with rice.

Freezable: Once cooled, freeze in an airtight container for up to 3 months.

Boxing Day Bakes

D
use vegetable oil instead of butter, and dairy-free cream cheese, stirring in once the filling has slightly cooled

LL
use lactose-free cream cheese

F
use lactose-free cream cheese, a low FODMAP stock cube and carrots/parsnips for the leftover veg element

V
use crumbled leftover nut roast instead of the turkey meat and vegetarian stuffing

VE
combine the dairy-free and vegetarian advice and use a sweetened almond milk to glaze instead of egg

Makes 4 large bakes

Takes 40 minutes

- 2 x 280g (10oz) store-bought gluten-free puff pastry sheets
- 1 egg, beaten, to glaze

For the filling

- 1 tbsp butter
- 100g (3½oz) leftover cooked turkey, chopped into 1cm (½in) chunks
- 50g (1¾oz) leftover cooked carrots, parsnips or Brussels sprouts, roughly chopped
- 50g (1¾oz) leftover gluten-free pork stuffing, crumbled
- 1 tbsp gluten-free plain (all-purpose) flour or cornflour (cornstarch)
- 200ml (generous ¾ cup) gluten-free chicken or ham stock
- 3 tbsp cream cheese
- ½ tsp salt
- ¼ tsp ground black pepper

Freezable: Once cooled, freeze in an airtight container for up to 3 months.

While everyone else seems to be enjoying festive variations of their favourite bakes, us gluten-free folks are still stuck with the same option bakeries provide us all year round... absolutely nothing! So take matters into your own hands and make these creamy turkey and stuffing bakes. Using store-bought gluten-free puff pastry makes this a breeze, and even a modest amount of leftovers goes a long way here.

1 Remove the pastry sheets from the fridge while you prepare the filling; this makes them easier to unroll without breaking or cracking.

2 Add the butter to a large saucepan and place over a medium heat. Once melted, add the turkey, vegetables and stuffing. Add the flour and stir until it disappears. Pour in the stock and cream cheese, then add the salt and pepper. Simmer until the liquid reduces to a thick sauce, then remove from the heat.

3 Preheat the oven to 200°C fan / 220°C / 425°F. Line a large baking tray with non-stick baking parchment.

4 Unroll one sheet of puff pastry on a flat work surface and transfer to a large sheet of non-stick baking parchment. Cut in half vertically and horizontally so you have 4 rectangles.

5 Brush the edges of two of the rectangles with beaten egg, then place a quarter of the filling in the centre of both rectangles, ensuring it doesn't touch the beaten egg. Next, place the other rectangles of pastry on top, gently pressing down around the edges. Use a fork to crimp and seal the edges. Transfer both bakes to the prepared baking tray, then repeat with the other sheet of puff pastry and the remaining filling.

6 At this point, you can lightly score lines in the top of the pastry using a small, sharp knife (ensuring you don't actually cut through the pastry) for the ultimate finishing touch. Brush all the bakes well with beaten egg.

7 Bake for 15 minutes until showing signs of turning golden, then cover with foil and bake for a further 5 minutes. They should look wonderfully golden and puffy when done.

Bubble and Squeak

D
use dairy-free 'buttery' margarine

LL

F
use only the green parts of the leek instead of onion

V
swap the turkey for leftover nut roast or 100g (3½oz) toasted pine nuts and use gluten-free veggie/vegan stuffing

VE
combine the dairy-free and vegetarian advice and omit the fried eggs

Serves 6

Takes 20 minutes

- 500g (1lb 2oz) leftover roast potatoes
- 300g (10½oz) leftover cooked carrots and parsnips
- 150g (5oz) leftover Brussels sprouts, roughly chopped
- 200g (7oz) leftover gluten-free pork stuffing, crumbled, or pigs in blankets, thinly sliced
- 150g (5oz) leftover cooked turkey, finely diced
- 4 tbsp cranberry sauce, plus extra to serve
- 2 tbsp butter
- 1 small leek or onion, finely chopped
- 6 eggs, fried in oil, to serve

Tip: Don't have any leftover turkey? Simply bulk it out with more leftovers or omit entirely.

If you've got a healthy amount of leftovers, you can easily use them all up the old-school British way: by mashing them together to create bubble and squeak. It's essentially a large, shareable potato cake that's packed with festive veggies, cranberry sauce, leftover turkey and stuffing, served with a fried egg on top. The outside is crisp and golden, while the inside is a chunky melting pot of Christmas dinner flavours.

1 Place the roast potatoes in a large mixing bowl and use a potato masher to break them up as much as possible, exposing the fluffy middle. Add the carrots and parsnips, sprouts, stuffing/pigs in blankets, diced turkey and cranberry sauce.

2 Again, use the potato masher to break up everything as much as possible, occasionally mixing to ensure that nothing escapes the wrath of your potato masher.

3 Preheat the grill (broiler) to a medium heat.

4 Place a large ovenproof frying pan or skillet over a medium heat, then add the butter. Once melted, add the leek or onion and fry until softened. Add to the bowl of leftovers and mix in well. Add the bowl of mashed leftovers to the pan and compact down into an even, flat layer. If your pan isn't quite big enough to comfortably accommodate it all, I'd recommend making two smaller bubble and squeak cakes instead.

5 Fry for 3–4 minutes before mixing everything up with a wooden spoon and compacting down again. Fry for a further 3–4 minutes.

6 Place the pan under the grill for 4–5 minutes or until the top has developed a lovely golden brown colour. Remove from the grill and place a large plate on top, then (with oven gloves on) quickly flip the whole thing so that the bubble and squeak is perfectly plated.

7 Allow to cool and firm up a little for 5–10 minutes before slicing and serving with fried eggs and a little more cranberry sauce on top.

Boxing Day Quiche

D
use dairy-free cream, milk and a smoked cheese that melts well

LL
use lactose-free cream and milk

F
use lactose-free cream and milk

V
use 100g (3½oz) leftover broccoli instead of pigs in blankets and turkey and ensure all cheese used is veggie-friendly

Serves 6

Takes 1 hour

- 1 quantity of ultimate gluten-free shortcrust pastry (page 204, or use store-bought)
- 75ml (⅓ cup) milk
- 175ml (¾ cup) double (heavy) cream
- 2 large eggs
- ½ tsp each of salt and ground black pepper
- 6–7 leftover gluten-free pigs in blankets, thinly sliced
- 50g (1¾oz) leftover cooked turkey, diced
- 5–6 leftover cooked Brussels sprouts, roughly chopped
- 100g (3½oz) leftover hard cheese from the cheeseboard, grated (Cheddar, Stilton, Wensleydale and Red Leicester work well)
- Cranberry sauce, to serve

Nothing gives a new lease of life to leftovers quite like my Boxing Day quiche. Best of all, a small amount of leftovers goes a long way here, so it's absolutely perfect if your food went down too well the day before! Buttery, golden, flaky pastry hosts a beautiful creamy, cheesy filling that's packed with pigs in blankets, turkey and chopped sprouts. But feel free to use whatever you have left over, as long as they're well chopped up.

1 Remove the pastry from the fridge; if it feels really firm, leave it out at room temperature briefly before rolling it.

2 Remember not to handle the dough excessively as you work with it, as this will warm it up and make it more fragile. Lightly flour your rolling pin. On a large sheet of non-stick baking parchment, roll out the dough to a 2mm (⅛in) thickness, in a large circular shape.

3 Transfer the pastry to a 23cm (9in) fluted tart tin (pan). I do this by supporting the pastry as I gently invert it into the tin, with equal overhang on all sides. Peel off the baking parchment.

4 Next, use your fingers to carefully ease the pastry into place, so that it neatly lines the tin. Lift the overhanging pastry and, using your thumb, squash 2mm (⅛in) of pastry back into the tin. This will result in slightly thicker sides, which will prevent the pastry case from shrinking when baked. Allow the overhang to do its thing – we'll trim the overhang after chilling it. Lightly prick the base of the pastry case with a fork, then place into the fridge for 15 minutes.

5 Preheat the oven to 180°C fan / 200°C / 400°F. Place a large baking tray in the oven

6 Use a rolling pin to roll over the top of the tin, instantly removing the overhang and flattening down the pastry.

Continued...

7 Next, loosely line the base of the pastry case with baking parchment and fill with baking beans (or uncooked rice if you don't have any). Place on the hot baking tray in the oven and cook for 15 minutes. Remove the baking parchment and baking beans, then bake for a further 5 minutes.

8 Meanwhile, in a large jug (pitcher), beat together the milk, cream and eggs, then season with the salt and pepper. Remove the pastry case and the hot baking tray from the oven. Work quickly from this point so the baking tray doesn't lose its heat!

9 Spread the sliced pigs in blankets, diced turkey, chopped sprouts and three-quarters of the grated cheese across the base of the pastry case.

10 Pour the egg mixture into the pastry case, then top with the remaining grated cheese. Carefully slide the quiche back into the preheated oven (ensuring you don't spill any!) and bake for 25 minutes. Once cooked, it should look lovely and golden brown on top, a little risen and not 'jiggly'.

11 Allow to cool for 5 minutes before removing from the tin and serving warm with a dollop of cranberry sauce on the side, if you like.

CHEESEBOARD
Mac 'n' cheese

D use a dairy-free 'buttery' margarine, milk and a smoked cheese that melts well

LL use lactose-free milk

 F use lactose-free milk

V ensure all cheese used is veggie-friendly

VE see dairy-free advice

Serves 4–5

Takes 30 minutes

- 400g (14oz) dried gluten-free macaroni
- 3 tbsp butter
- 2 tbsp cornflour (cornstarch)
- 400ml (1⅔ cups) milk
- 1 tbsp Dijon mustard
- 100g (3½oz) Stilton, crumbled
- 50g (1¾oz) extra-mature Cheddar, grated
- 50g (1¾oz) red Leicester, grated
- 50g (1¾oz) Wensleydale with cranberries, crumbled
- ½ tsp salt
- ½ tsp ground black pepper
- 4–5 gluten-free oatcakes or crackers, roughly chopped
- Small handful of fresh sage, finely chopped

This recipe is perfect for using up small amounts of leftover cheese and crackers from the previous day's cheeseboard. Though I've provided my ideal combination of cheese below (the resulting sauce is an absolute dream), feel free to use similar amounts of whatever cheeses you have left over.

1 Preheat the oven to 200°C fan / 220°C / 425°F.

2 Cook the macaroni according to the package instructions - gluten-free pasta can often clump together, so adding a teaspoon of oil to the water, as well as a teaspoon of salt, can massively help prevent this. You want to err on the undercooked side, as the pasta will cook further in the oven.

3 While the pasta is cooking, place a large ovenproof frying pan or skillet over a medium heat, then add the butter. Once melted, add the cornflour and mix together using a wooden spoon until it forms a smooth paste without lumps. Pour in the milk and mix constantly until it forms a nice, smooth sauce. Take off the heat.

4 Add the mustard and all the cheeses and stir until melted, then season with the salt and pepper.

5 Drain the macaroni and add to the pan. Mix until well coated in the sauce. Spread everything out in the pan so it's all in an even, flat layer. If you're not using an ovenproof frying pan or skillet, pour the contents of your pan into an ovenproof dish (roughly 33 x 28cm / 13 x 11in) and spread out into a flat layer.

6 Combine the chopped oatcakes and sage, then scatter evenly over the top. Place in the oven for 15 minutes or until the top is golden and crisp.

Freezable: Once cooled, freeze in an airtight container for up to 3 months.

Mark's Pigs in Blankets Chow Mein

 D

 LF

 F
serve no more than 50g (1¾oz) per person

 V
use 3–4 slices of leftover nut roast (chopped) instead of pigs in blankets, being careful not to break it up too much when stir-frying

 VE
see vegetarian advice

Serves 2–3

Takes 15 minutes

- 200g (7oz) dried ribbon rice noodles
- 4 tbsp gluten-free soy sauce
- 2 tsp black treacle
- 1 tsp brown sugar
- 1 tsp cornflour (cornstarch)
- 2 tsp sesame oil
- 1 tbsp garlic-infused oil
- 10–12 leftover gluten-free pigs in blankets, thinly sliced
- 200g (7oz) leftover cooked carrots, parsnips or Brussels sprouts, roughly chopped
- Big handful of beansprouts
- Small handful of spring onion (scallion) greens, chopped, plus extra to serve

This is Mark's go-to stir-fry recipe whenever he's using up leftovers – using rice noodles for me, of course! His combination of gluten-free soy sauce, black treacle, brown sugar and cornflour is his own creation that forges a gluten-free combo of kecap manis and dark gluten-free soy sauce right there in the wok. The result is a sweet, sticky and savoury stir-fry that is absolutely out of this world with Christmas leftovers.

1 Prepare the dried rice noodles according to the package instructions. Mark places his in a heatproof bowl, adds boiling water from the kettle and covers with a plate for 5 minutes. Drain and set aside.

2 Combine the soy sauce, treacle, sugar, cornflour and sesame oil together in a small dish. Mix until combined and without lumps, and set aside.

3 Add the garlic-infused oil to a wok and place over a medium-high heat. Once hot, add the pigs in blankets and vegetables and stir-fry for 2 minutes.

4 Add the drained noodles and prepared sauce – the sauce should sizzle. Stir-fry until everything is well coated and the sauce has reduced to a nice, sticky coating. Add the beansprouts and push them underneath the noodles to allow them to wilt for 1–2 minutes, then add the chopped spring onion greens and toss.

5 Remove from the heat, garnish with a few more spring onion greens and serve.

Tip: I'd highly recommend using flat rice noodles that contain tapioca starch for this dish as, not only do they not break as easily, but they also have a texture that's much closer to egg noodles. You'll also find a recipe for gluten-free egg noodles in my first book, *How To Make Anything Gluten-free*.

BOXING DAY
Puff Pastry Pie

 use a dairy-free 'buttery' margarine and dairy-free cream instead of cream cheese

 use lactose-free cream cheese

 use lactose-free cream cheese, only the green parts of the leek instead of onion and a low FODMAP stock cube

Serves 6–8

Takes 45 minutes

- 1 x 280g (10oz) store-bought gluten-free puff pastry sheet
- 2 tbsp butter
- 1 small onion or ½ leek, finely chopped
- 300g (10½oz) leftover carrots, parsnips or Brussels sprouts, roughly chopped
- 1 tbsp gluten-free plain (all-purpose) flour or cornflour (cornstarch)
- 500ml (generous 2 cups) chicken stock
- 300–400g (10½–14oz) leftover cooked turkey, chopped into bite-sized chunks
- 5 leftover gluten-free pork stuffing balls or 200g (7oz) ham, crumbled or diced into 1cm (½in) chunks
- 2 tbsp finely chopped roasting herbs (rosemary, thyme, sage)
- Pinch each of salt and ground black pepper
- 2 tbsp cream cheese
- 1 egg, beaten

Fancy using up all your leftovers in one fell swoop? If so, this puff pastry-topped pie with a bold, creamy filling is perfect for you. All you need to do is simply whip up my ultimate leftovers pie filling (which only takes around 10 minutes to make), top with pastry and bake.

1 Preheat the oven to 180°C fan / 200°C / 400°F. Remove the pastry sheet from the fridge – this makes it easier to unroll without it breaking or cracking.

2 Place a large pan over a medium heat and add the butter. Once melted, add the onion or leek and fry until softened. Add the leftover veggies and fry for a further 3 minutes, then add the flour and mix until it disappears. Pour in the stock and simmer until it thickens a little, then add the turkey, stuffing/ham, roasting herbs and salt and pepper. Stir, then add the cream cheese and mix until a thick, creamy sauce is formed.

3 Pour the filling mixture into a 28 x 23cm (11 x 9in) rectangular pie dish (any pie dish smaller than your puff pastry sheet will do, as long as it's not too deep) and brush the edges of the dish with beaten egg. Lay the sheet of pastry perfectly on top and gently press down around the edges. Press 1cm (½in) of overhang back on itself, then trim away any excess pastry and crimp the edges with a fork.

4 Score wavy lines in the pastry lid using a sharp knife (but don't cut through the lid!) and brush with beaten egg. Bake in the oven for 30 minutes, covering loosely with foil after 15 minutes once it's golden brown. Allow to cool for 5–10 minutes before slicing and serving with gluten-free gravy, cranberry sauce and mashed potato.

Freezable: Once cooled, divide into individual portions and freeze in airtight containers for up to 3 months.

CHOCOLATE BOX

Rocky Road

D — use a hard dairy-free alternative to butter and dairy-free chocolate(s)

LL — use lactose-free chocolate(s)

F — see low lactose advice and ensure any leftover chocolates used are FODMAP friendly

V — use veggie-friendly mini marshmallows

VE — see dairy-free advice and use mini vegan marshmallows

Makes 16 small or 9 large squares

Takes 20 minutes + chilling

- 150g (5oz) gluten-free digestive biscuits (graham crackers)
- 200–250g (7–9oz) leftover chocolates (ensure gluten-free)
- 300g (10½oz) 54% or 74% dark chocolate, broken by hand
- 150g (⅔ cup) butter, plus extra for greasing
- 4 tbsp golden syrup
- 70g (2½oz) mini marshmallows, plus an extra 30g (1oz) to scatter on top

Freezable: Once sliced, freeze in an airtight container for up to 2 months.

For those who have never experienced it before, 'leftover chocolate' is chocolate that *didn't* get eaten. Shocking, I know. But even if you find yourself lacking enough leftover chocolates at Christmas, it's well worth diligently squirrelling a few handfuls away purely to make this. I use some of the well-known chocolate assortment boxes and tins here in the UK, which are commonly gluten-free, giving you a surprise in every bite.

1 Grease a 20cm (8in) square baking tin (pan) and line with non-stick baking parchment, allowing the paper to overhang so it's easier to lift out later.

2 Place the biscuits in a zip-lock bag and bash with a rolling pin until broken into chunks, but not a fine powder! Use a large knife to chop 125g (4½oz) of the leftover chocolates into small chunks, placing the rest to one side.

3 Add the dark chocolate, butter and syrup to a large heatproof bowl. Half fill a saucepan with boiling water, place over a medium heat and bring to a simmer. Place the bowl on top of the pan of simmering water and heat for 3–4 minutes, stirring occasionally, until everything is melted and combined.

4 Once melted, use a large spoon to remove 100g (3½oz) of the mixture. To reduce the likelihood of drizzling chocolate all over the stove top, I first put a small bowl on my digital scales and set it to zero. Next, I move the bowl over the melted mixture, add in a spoonful and then return it to the scale to check the measurement until reaching the right weight. Place to one side.

5 Take the pan off the heat and add the crushed biscuits to the large bowl of melted mixture; stir in well. Next, mix in the marshmallows and chopped leftover chocolates and stir in once more.

6 Bring the baking tin close to the bowl of rocky road mixture, then lift the bowl (oven gloves are advised) and pour it into the tin. Spread the mixture out and compact it down well before pouring the reserved melted mixture on top and spreading into an even, flat layer.

7 Gently press the reserved whole chocolates into the surface and scatter the extra mini marshmallows around the chocolates.

8 Chill in the fridge for 2–3 hours until firm. Use the baking parchment to lift the rocky road out onto a work surface and, using a large, sharp knife, cut into 16 small or 9 large squares; running the knife under a hot tap for 20–30 seconds can help massively if you've allowed it to chill longer than stated.

Chocolate Box Brownies

 D use dairy-free chocolate, chocolate chips and Christmas chocolates

 LL use lactose-free chocolate, chocolate chips and Christmas chocolates

 V

Makes 9–16

Takes 45 minutes

- 250g (9oz) dark chocolate, broken into pieces
- 250g (1 cup plus 2 tbsp) butter, plus extra for greasing
- 100g (¾ cup) gluten-free plain (all-purpose) flour
- 50g (½ cup) unsweetened cocoa powder
- 4 medium or 3 large eggs
- 280g (1½ cups minus 2 tbsp) caster (superfine) sugar
- 60g (2oz) white chocolate chips
- 120g (4oz) leftover Christmas chocolates, plus an extra 100g (3½oz) for the top

Freezable: Once cooled and sliced, freeze in an airtight container for up to 3 months.

Though these brownies are mind-blowing enough without them, something magical happens when you throw in the remnants of a chocolate selection box. Each slice is a bit of a mystery as to what you'll find in terms of taste and texture, making these super-fudgy, chocolatey brownies even more enjoyable to eat than they already were.

1 Preheat the oven to 160°C fan / 180°C / 350°F. Grease and line a 23cm (9in) square baking tin (pan) with non-stick baking parchment.

2 Add the chocolate and butter to a large heatproof bowl. Half fill a large saucepan with boiling water, place over a medium heat and bring to a simmer. Place the bowl on top of the saucepan of simmering water and stir until everything has melted and mixed together. Remove the bowl from the pan and leave to cool to near room temperature.

3 Sift the flour and cocoa powder into a medium bowl and mix.

4 In a large mixing bowl, whisk the eggs with the sugar until paler – I prefer to use an electric hand whisk or a stand mixer for this. Pour the now cooled, melted chocolate mixture into the egg and sugar mixture. Carefully fold it in with a spatula until glossy.

5 Add the flour and cocoa mixture to the bowl and fold in until well combined. Fold in the white chocolate chips and leftover Christmas chocolates so that they're evenly distributed.

6 Spoon the mixture into the prepared baking tin, smoothing it over to create a nice, even layer. Bake in the oven for 35–40 minutes until it develops a shiny, paper-like crust on top. As soon as it comes out of the oven, push the extra Christmas chocolates into the top.

7 Allow to cool in the tin briefly, then carefully lift onto a cooling rack. Once fully cooled, cut into squares and enjoy.

Christmas Aftermath Ice Cream

Makes 1 litre (4 cups)

Takes 10 minutes
+ 8 hours chilling

- 600ml (2½ cups) double (heavy) cream
- 1 x 397g (14oz) can of condensed milk
- 2 tsp vanilla extract
- 80ml (⅓ cup) rum (optional)
- 300g (10½oz) leftover Christmas pudding, Christmas cake or Dundee cake, crumbled, plus an extra 100g (3½oz) to scatter on top (see pages 172, 56 or 59 for homemade, or use store-bought but ensure gluten-free)
- 100ml (generous ⅓ cup) caramel
- 200g (7oz) leftover festive biscuits (cookies), chopped into 1cm (½in) chunks

This is my favourite use of sweet festive leftovers, including Christmas cake and leftover biscuits or cookies (I use gingerbread), which pair so well with my gluten-free brandy snap baskets (page 146). The rum, when combined with the Christmas cake, gives the entire thing a rum and raisin flavour that I am positively addicted to. Of course, it works just as well without the rum too, so feel free to mix and match the cake and biscuits you use to create your own flavour combinations.

1 Line 2 x 450g (1lb) loaf tins (pans) with non-stick baking parchment.

2 Place the cream, condensed milk, vanilla extract and rum, if using, in a large mixing bowl or the bowl of a stand mixer. Use an electric hand mixer to combine all of the ingredients or use the balloon whisk attachment on the stand mixer on a slow speed to mix until combined.

3 Increase the speed to high and mix until it thickens and soft peaks are formed. Add the crumbled Christmas pudding, cake or Dundee cake and stir in gently by hand using a silicone spatula, until evenly dispersed.

4 Spoon a quarter of the mixture into each tin and gently smooth it over using the spatula. Drizzle a quarter of the caramel and scatter a quarter of the chopped leftover biscuits on top of both. Divide the remaining whipped cream mixture between both tins and smooth over, before topping with the remaining caramel and leftover chopped biscuits. Finally, sprinkle the extra Christmas pudding, cake or Dundee cake on top and gently push any large chunks in.

5 Place in the freezer for 8 hours or overnight. Remove from the freezer 5–10 minutes before serving, in gluten-free ice-cream cones or my brandy snap baskets (page 146).

Tip: If you don't have two 450g (1lb) loaf tins, you can always use a singular 900g (2lb) loaf tin instead.

Leftover Panettone Bread and Butter Pudding

V

Serves 6–8

Takes 40 minutes

- 450g (1lb) leftover gluten-free panettone (see page 36 for homemade, or use store-bought), cut into thin wedges
- 70g (⅓ cup) butter, softened
- 3 large eggs
- 225ml (1 cup minus 1 tbsp) double (heavy) cream
- 225ml (1 cup minus 1 tbsp) whole milk
- 50g (¼ cup) caster (superfine) sugar
- 1 tbsp dark rum (optional)
- 1 tsp vanilla extract
- 50g (1¾oz) dark chocolate chips (optional)
- 20g (scant 2 tbsp) demerara (turbinado) sugar

It's easy over Christmas with more food around than usual, and generally just a messier kitchen, to forget about things you may have opened and not finished. I've found this with gluten-free panettone in the past and refuse to waste a single scrap of it. The best solution when it's a little bit past its best? Bread and butter pudding! This recipe is so delicious you could just make/buy panettone specifically to turn it into this.

1 Preheat the oven to 160°C fan / 180°C / 350°F. Lightly grease a 33 x 28cm (13 x 11in) oven dish with butter.

2 Lightly butter one side of each slice of panettone and then cut into slightly smaller pieces and layer into the dish.

3 In a large mixing bowl, combine the eggs, cream, milk, caster sugar, rum, if using, and vanilla extract. Pour over the top of the panettone and allow to soak for 5–10 minutes.

4 Sprinkle the chocolate chips over the top, followed by the demerara sugar. Bake in the oven for 30 minutes until the top is slightly crisp and the custard beneath is set.

5 Serve hot or cold with cream or gluten-free custard.

Tip: If you don't have enough panettone (or any at all!) use leftover gluten-free bread instead. If choosing to add alcohol, feel free to use brandy or whisky instead.

Freezable: Once cooled, slice into individual portions and freeze in airtight containers for up to 3 months.

Essentials

Choux Pastry

Makes 38–40 profiteroles
Takes 30 minutes

This is the same, reliable gluten-free choux pastry recipe you'll find in my second book *How To Bake Anything Gluten Free* but doubled, simply because that's how much you'll need for my profiterole wreath recipe over on page 168. Please remember that you might not need all of the egg, as it can make the dough way too runny to be piped; so add it slowly and stop when you've achieved a consistency that can hold its shape well.

- 300g (2¼ cups) gluten-free plain (all-purpose) flour
- 1 tsp xanthan gum
- 4 tsp caster (superfine) sugar
- ½ tsp salt
- 300ml (1¼ cups) milk
- 300ml (1¼ cups) water
- 200g (7oz) butter, cubed
- 6–7 large eggs, beaten

1 Sift the flour, xanthan gum, sugar and salt into a large mixing bowl. Place to one side.

2 Add the milk, water and cubed butter to a large saucepan and place over a low to medium heat. Gently heat until the butter has melted, then bring to a gentle simmer and, as soon as it is simmering, take off the heat and immediately add your dry mixture to the pan. Mix immediately and vigorously until everything comes together into a dough that almost resembles mashed potato. Place your pan back onto a medium heat for 2–4 minutes, stirring until it forms more of a ball and releases more moisture. We don't want the mixture to be super wet, but of course, don't let it stick to the bottom of the pan!

3 Place the dough in a large mixing bowl and allow to cool for 10–15 minutes. Once cooled, add your beaten eggs a little at a time to the dough, mixing thoroughly between each addition until smooth. Watch the consistency of the dough as you add the egg, as you don't want it to go too runny - it needs to be thick enough to be a pipeable consistency that can hold its shape, and you might not need all of the egg. You can mix in the egg by hand using a wooden spoon quite easily but it's a proper workout! I use an electric hand whisk on a low speed.

4 Transfer the dough to a piping bag fitted with a 1cm (½in) round nozzle.

Ultimate Shortcrust Pastry

Makes 560g (1lb 4oz)
Takes 15 minutes
+ 30 minutes chilling

This is my favourite gluten-free pastry recipe. It's so easy to work with that you'll forget about all those failed gluten-free pastry attempts in an instant. You'll need this for my mince pie pop tarts (page 70), salted caramel and pear frangipane tart (page 159), pecan pie (page 177), broccoli and cauliflower cheese tart (page 131) and Boxing Day quiche (page 187).

- 300g (2¼ cups) gluten-free plain (all-purpose) flour
- 1½ tsp xanthan gum
- 145g (⅔ cup) very cold butter, cut into 1cm (½in) cubes
- 3 tbsp caster (superfine) sugar (for sweet pastry only)
- 1 tsp salt (for savoury pastry only)
- 2 large eggs, beaten

1 In a large mixing bowl, mix together the flour and xanthan gum. Make sure your butter is really cold; if not, put it in the fridge or freezer until nicely chilled. Add the cubes to the bowl and, using your fingertips, rub the butter into the flour until it has a breadcrumb-like consistency. Make sure your hands are cool, as we want to avoid the butter getting warm! (You can also achieve the same result by using a food processor to blitz the ingredients together.)

2 If making sweet pastry, stir in the sugar, or if making savoury pastry, stir in the salt.

3 Add the beaten egg and, using a knife, carefully cut it into the mixture until it comes together. It should form a ball and not be crumbly – it will be a little sticky to touch but not unmanageable.

4 Wrap the dough in cling film (plastic wrap) and leave to chill in the fridge for around 30 minutes before using. You can freeze this pastry for up to 2 months; defrost fully before using.

Tip: Chill! Using cold butter and chilling the dough makes your gluten-free pastry stronger and more workable. Making any type of pastry on an incredibly hot day isn't advisable, as the warmer your dough is, the more fragile it will become. However, make sure once chilled, you allow your pastry to warm up a bit before rolling, otherwise it will crack.

Gluten-Free Self-Raising (Self-Rising) Flour

Makes about 500g (3 cups)
Takes 2 minutes

Gluten-free self-raising flour is readily available across all supermarkets in the UK. But if you can't find it where you live, you can easily make your own using the ratios below.

• 500g (3¾ cups) gluten-free plain (all-purpose) flour
• 6 tsp gluten-free baking powder
• 1 tsp xanthan gum

1 Simply combine all the ingredients in a large mixing bowl and mix thoroughly, then store in a large airtight container. Consider labelling it so you can tell it apart from other flour.

2 Use whenever a recipe calls for gluten-free self-raising flour.

Gluten-Free Plain (all-purpose) Flour

Makes 1kg (7½ cups)
Takes 2 minutes

If you live in the UK, you can easily find gluten-free plain (all-purpose) flour in supermarkets; in which case, you don't need this recipe! This recipe is for anyone who can't easily source gluten-free plain flour where they live or for anyone who has had mixed results using their country's equivalent. As commercial blends contain flours/starches in specific quantities, they can vary wildly depending on where you live in the world – and so can your baking results. So here's a blend you can rely on for using in this book – you can easily purchase these starches and flours online.

• 500g (3 cups) rice flour
• 150g (1 cup) tapioca starch
• 150g (¾ cup) potato starch
• 150g (1¼ cups) cornflour (cornstarch)
• 50g (scant ½ cup) buckwheat flour

1 Simply combine all the ingredients in a large mixing bowl and mix thoroughly, then store in a large airtight container. Consider labelling it so you can tell it apart from other flour!

2 Use whenever a recipe calls for gluten-free plain flour.

Tip: Ensure all the flours and starches that you use for the blend do not have 'may contain' warnings for gluten. I find this is especially relevant when sourcing tapioca starch and buckwheat flour.

Don't Forget About These!

In case you didn't know, this is the fifth gluten-free book I've written and, in an effort to provide as much value as possible, I strive to never repeat recipes across my books unless absolutely necessary.

What that does mean, however, is that there are tons more recipes in my previous books that would be absolutely perfect for Christmas (like my classic key lime pie, my Auntie Carol's trifle, tiramisu and more) that you won't find in this book. So to ensure you're aware of that and don't forget about them (because having a choice as a gluten-free person is so rare!) I've decided to list them here, so you know exactly in which book to find them. After all, *How to Bake Anything Gluten Free* even has it's own Christmas chapter!

While some of these recipes might not immediately seem overtly Christmas related, when you think about Christmas day breakfast, party food and dessert, you'll soon understand why I've given them a shout out.

Also don't forget that my blog (glutenfreecuppatea.co.uk) has even more festive recipes on it that I've built up over the past ten years.

How to Make Anything Gluten Free

How to Bake Anything Gluten Free

How to Plan Anything Gluten Free

Quick and Easy Gluten Free

Index

c

EGG CONVERSION GUIDE

Did you know that a large egg in the UK is actually bigger than in the USA, Canada and Australia? Me neither! That's why I thought I'd pop in a handy egg conversion guide in the back of this book to help make things simple.

That way, when a recipe calls for a small, medium or large egg, you can use the table below to work out exactly what that means for you. I've used UK egg sizes in all my recipes, so just convert from there.

	UK	USA	Canada	Australia
Small	53g and under	42.5g / 1½oz	42g / 1½oz	N/A
Medium	53–63g	49.6g / 1¾oz	49g / 1¾oz	43g
Large	63–73g	56.7g / 2oz	56g / 2oz	52g
Extra large	73g and over	63.8g / 2¼oz	63g / 2¼oz	60g
Jumbo	N/A	70.9g / 2½oz	70g / 2½oz	68g

And just in case you're too lazy to look at anything presented in a table (like I am), here's your cheat sheet! Maybe we can call a meeting of all our world leaders and agree on a uniform egg size in future?

So when a recipe in this book calls for a **small egg**, you should use a:

USA: medium egg
Canada: medium egg
Australia: large egg

When a recipe in this book calls for a **medium egg**, you should use a:

USA: large egg
Canada: large egg
Australia: extra-large egg

When a recipe in this book calls for a **large egg**, you should use a:

USA: extra-large egg
Canada: extra-large egg.
Australia: jumbo egg

GAS MARK CONVERSION GUIDE

Here's a helpful table for oven temperature conversions depending on the kind of oven you use.

Celsius (fan)	Celsius	Fahrenheit	Gas mark
100	120	250	½
120	140	285	1
130	150	300	2
140	160	325	3
160	180	350	4
170	190	375	5
180	200	400	6
200	220	425	7
210	230	450	8
230	250	480	9
240	260	500	10

Thank you

Though I'm still in overwhelming disbelief that this is my fifth book, I probably shouldn't be when considering the awesome team of expert Christmas elves who made it possible.

A hearty yuletide thanks to the 'Quad Squad' at Quadrille Publishing and Sarah Lavelle for everything along this crazy journey so far (especially Sarah's patience with me!) and for being so on board with this book. Thanks to my editor Harriet Webster for all her genius, hard work and support (on and off the page) and thank you yet again to my diligent copy editor, Sally Somers.

I can't thank Emily Lapworth enough for her wonderful festive design that undeniably spreads Christmas cheer across each page of this book. Thank you once again to Hannah Hughes for the truly mouth-watering food photography - even Santa would have no idea that everything pictured is gluten-free! Thank you to Amy Stephenson, Valeria Russo and Sophie Pryn for their wondrous food-styling and Rebecca Newport for the lavish, tinsel-tinged prop styling.

Thank you to Cat Parnell for her hair and make-up magic on set and Nicky for always going out of her way to cut and colour my hair whenever I have a book shoot coming up! Thank you once again to Amy for all your joyous, Christmas-themed nail art skills.

Thanks to 'Team Laura' (Laura Willis and Laura Eldridge), Ruth Tewkesbury and Iman Khabl for championing this book and ensuring gluten-free food also gets the coverage it needs and deserves.

Thanks to my boyfriend, Mark, for sharing his own recipes and his dedication to recipe/taste testing, which included eating Christmas cake and mince pies in the heat of mid-July. Woof-woof to all the furry friends who acted as enthusiastic mascots during the creation of this book, including Peggy (I know you can't read, but you keep me sane!), Ned, Marie and Oscar.

Thank you to my Mum and Dad, Charlie, Gemma and the Farrow clan, as well as Mark's family, for all the unyielding support and taste-testing.

And last but definitely not least: thanks a million to all my dedicated followers (shoutout to the Facebook group!) and readers for the seemingly endless support and positivity across all of my books so far. I hope this book helps to bring back that Christmas magic that, if you were like me, you may have long forgotten about.

About the Author

Becky Excell is a best-selling author and gluten-free food writer with a following of over 1 million on her social media channels and over 1 million monthly views on her award-winning blog, which recently celebrated it's 10th birthday.

She won the Observer Food Monthly's Best Food Personality award in 2022, as well as the Blogosphere Award's Food Creator of the Year.

She's been eating gluten-free for nearly 15 years and writes recipes for numerous print and online publications. She has made various TV appearances, showing the nation how easy it is to make delicious gluten-free food, as well as cooking and baking at events including the BBC Good Food Show and The Big Feastival.

She gave up a career working in PR and marketing to focus on food full-time, with an aim to develop recipes which reunite her and her followers with the foods they can no longer eat. Her first four *Sunday Times* best-selling cookbooks, *How to Make Anything Gluten Free*, *How to Bake Anything Gluten Free*, *How to Plan Anything Gluten Free* and *Quick and Easy Gluten Free*, were published by Quadrille. She lives in Essex, UK.

Managing Director
Sarah Lavelle

Commissioning Editor
Harriet Webster

Copy Editor
Sally Somers

Art Direction and Design
Emily Lapworth

Assistant Designer
Gemma Hayden

Typesetter
Jonathan Baker, Seagull Design

Photographer
Hannah Hughes

Food Stylist
Amy Stephenson

Prop Stylist
Rebecca Newport

Make-up Artist
Cat Parnell

Head of Production
Stephen Lang

Senior Production Controller
Sabeena Atchia

First published in 2023 by
Quadrille, an imprint of
Hardie Grant Publishing

Quadrille
52–54 Southwark Street
London SE1 1UN
quadrille.com

Text © Becky Excell 2023
Photography © Hannah Hughes 2023
Design and layout © Quadrille 2023

Cataloguing in Publication Data:
a catalogue record for this book
is available from the British Library.

Reprinted in 2023
10 9 8 7 6 5 4 3 2

UK ISBN: 978 1 83783 120 3
US + AUS ISBN: 978 1 78713 827 8

Printed in Germany by Firmengruppe
Appl in Wemding

Many thanks to **Le Creuset**,
Meri Meri and **Talking Tables**,
who kindly donated ceramics,
cookware and props for the
photoshoot.

MIX
Paper | Supporting
responsible forestry
FSC® C004592
FSC
www.fsc.org

This book is not intended
as a substitute for genuine medical
advice. The reader should consult
a medical professional in matters relating
to their health, particularly with regard
to symptoms of IBS and coeliac disease.

FODMAP information was correct at
the time of writing, but please check the
Monash University FODMAP app for
the latest information on serving sizes.
These may change via updates
in the future.